Logging Railroads of the Saco River Valley

Logging Railroads
of the
Saco River Valley

BILL GOVE

Bondcliff Books • Littleton, New Hampshire

Logging Railroads of the Saco River Valley
Copyright © 2001 by Bill Gove

Library of Congress Catalog Card Number 2001094347
ISBN 1–931271–02–X

Text composition by Passumpsic Publishing, St. Johnsbury, Vt.
Printed in the United States by Sherwin Dodge Printers, Littleton, N.H.

COVER PHOTO: The Conway Company's first Baldwin saddletank engine and crew,
mainstays of the Swift River Railroad.

Additional copies of this book may be obtained directly from:
Bondcliff Books
P.O. Box 385
Littleton, NH 03561

Contents

Introduction

The Saco River in southwestern Maine had the distinction during the early years of being in the center of the logging industry in the State. Stretching for 95 miles from the coastal communities of Biddeford and Saco, the meandering river courses northwesterly and northerly into New Hampshire, to a place of small beginnings in a narrow ravine in the White Mountains. The source is little Saco Lake in Crawford Notch. Flowing down through the once abundant white pine and red oak forests of southwestern Maine, the river once floated large quantities of logs to the many sawmills and shipyards on the lower stretches of the river, particularly in the Biddeford–Saco area near the mouth of the river.

Sawmilling had begun on the Saco River in the late 1600s, creating throughout the following century the largest lumbering activity in the entire state. Demand was greater than the available resource, however. The old-growth pine and oak were rapidly consumed by the shipbuilding and export industry. The loggers had no choice but to move further up the Saco River to find enough timber. Eventually reaching up to the Fryeburg area, the first river drive from there was in 1772. The woods of New Hampshire were just around the corner.

By the 1830s the Saco logging industry had shrunk to small proportions and paled next to the burgeoning activity in the woods along the Kennebec and Penobscot Rivers of Maine. With the decline of the large sawmills in the cities of Biddeford and Saco and the depletion of much of the pine, the last large timber cut in the Saco River valley was about 1877; the old growth white pine was gone.

Passing up the Saco River into the White Mountains of New Hampshire, the timber type changes. No longer dominated by white pine—that magnet that drew the loggers north along the Saco River—the timbered slopes of the White Mountains supported a forest of a different character. Dominant in the mountain forest was red spruce and the northern hardwoods of beech, birch, and maple.

During the 1800s spruce replaced the now less-abundant white pine as the preferred wood for construction lumber, and there was an abundant amount of spruce in those mountains of New Hampshire; an endless supply, it seemed to many. But driving logs down the river was not a practical solution for movement of the timber harvest from these remote mountain slopes and valleys, with streams too small to float a log.

Then along came the railroad loggers.

Acknowledgments

Many decades have passed since the little steam locomotives pounded their way along the crooked stream courses among the White Mountains, many decades that have seen interesting history forgotten and forever lost. But not entirely. Fortunately there have been a few old-timers with sharp memories that were able to share with me their remembrances of how life once was in the days of steam. Now even those few are gone, unfortunately.

Research for this volume began more than thirty years ago, when there were a few old-timers still around: men such as Harry Marsh and Eddie Parent, who worked on the Swift River and the Rocky Branch. And there were a few local residents whose memories stretched back to the early 1900s: men such as Maurice Lovejoy, William Oakes, Cliff Pratt, and a few others whose names have been lost in the time interval.

Gratitude is extended toward those whose efforts have preserved whatever is possible from the past, such as David Emerson of the Conway Historical Society, Bartlett librarian Jean Garland, and the archives from the New Hampshire Historical Society and the State Library. Thanks go to my many contemporaries whose generosity and assistance is appreciated, such as Peter Crane with his research material and photos; George Cook, who checked the map work; forest researcher Charles Cogbill; and railroad fan Ben English. From the White Mountain National Forest there was Karl Roenke and Steve Fay.

Many of the photographs came from the splendid collection of the late Lawrence Breed Walker, but thanks go to others from many years ago whose names have been lost in the shuffle.

Logging Railroads of the Saco River Valley

CHAPTER ONE

The Old-Growth Forests Along the Upper Saco River

DEVELOPMENT OF the lumber industry in northern New Hampshire came much later than it did along coastal Maine. The first settlement in the Conway, New Hampshire, area didn't occur until about 1764. And then it was not many years after this settlement that the large contingent of Saco River loggers arrived, seeking more white pine to feed the sawmill and shipbuilding industry at the mouth of the Saco.

There were some magnificent pine trees to be found along the river valleys, of course, but as the elevations increased sharply along the meandering streams, the timbermen found that the forest presented a different character. Red spruce, not pine, was the dominant softwood or coniferous tree. This meant a little different style of logging and a different market for the lumber.

The Old-Growth Forest of the White Mountains

The virgin forest in the mountains of northern New Hampshire had essentially the same tree species as one might encounter today. The proportions of each species, however, were different; spruce, for example, was much more plentiful than can be observed anywhere today in the White Mountains.

The variety of forest stands among the mountains and valleys was rarely homogeneous in composition or in age. Tree growth was slow except in spots

---

(Opposite page): An opening was created in this virgin stand of spruce when the overmature fir in the foreground died. The ground is covered with spruce and fir seedlings. The spruce tree with the axe stuck in it measured 18 inches in diameter. U.S. Forest Service photo

Hemlock trees predominate in this old-growth stand located on poorly drained soil in the Bartlett Experimental Forest. The age of the mature softwood trees was estimated to be 250 years or older. U.S. Forest Service photo

where the continual natural death and decay created openings. Occasional blowdowns in exposed areas and the infrequent fires would leave openings for new growth. The virgin timber stands in the White Mountains were, of course, quite picturesque to hike through, but they were not always productive or healthy forests.

To somewhat simplify the different forest types in this mountainous area of northern New Hampshire, one could classify three basic areas of timber growth: spruce flats, hardwood forests, and spruce slopes. The spruce flats, located at a low elevation that made them easily accessible, were the first areas to be harvested by the railroad loggers. The soil was moist and often shallow to the water table. Red spruce was the most adaptable species for the site, often comprising 80 percent of the stand. Although the poorly drained sites did not provide for optimum growth conditions, large spruce could be found as big as 20 inches in diameter (DBH). What white pine there might have been on these flats had probably been removed before the railroad loggers even appeared.

At a slightly higher elevation, there were the hardwood sites characterized by well-drained, deeper, richer soils. Beech was frequently the dominant hardwood species in the virgin forest of the White Mountains, often comprising a third of the trees on the hardwood sites. Hard maple and yellow birch were the other more common hardwoods, which made for a dense, clean forest with heavy shade. Tree sizes would vary up to diameters of 26 inches for beech, 30 inches for hard maple and 36 inches for yellow birch. There would usually be a small mixture of red spruce in with the dominant hardwoods, and it was on these rich hardwood sites that the most magnificent specimens of red spruce were found. These hardwood sites would extend up to about 2,200–2,400 feet in elevation on the mountainsides.

Up higher on the slopes, above an elevation of 2,400 feet, there was the spruce slope, with soil shallow to bedrock, and growing sites best suited again for red spruce along with balsam fir. On these slopes is where the loggers found the heaviest stands of mature spruce, often comprising 90 percent of the stand and reaching heights of 80 to 90 feet and diameters of 24 inches, and occasionally 30 inches. It was a dense growth with a typical stand exceeding 9,000 board feet of merchantable timber per acre. The age of the dominant trees varied from 200 to 390 years, occasionally older, but even the smaller trees in the under-story could be of an older age. Growth was often suppressed, almost stagnant, in the virgin forest, with its dense canopy overhead. Balsam fir might reach a maximum age of 150 years, but usually not much over 100.

These slopes covered with merchantable spruce would extend up to about 3,000–3,500 feet in elevation. Beyond that, the tree growth gradually merged into a growth of shorter spruce and fir, the fir becoming much more numerous along with some white birch, stunted yellow birch and other high-elevation plant life that was not considered merchantable by the lumbermen.

White pine was not plentiful on most of these mountain slopes but did

Beech predominates, but hard maple is common on this old-growth hardwood stand on the deep soils of a lower slope in the Bartlett Experimental Forest.
U.S. Forest Service photo

This virgin spruce stand on a White Mountain slope contained trees with diameters up to 28 inches and heights of 95 feet.
U.S. Forest Service photo

frequent the intervals and other sandy soils along the river courses. The Swift River, a tributary of the Saco, once had a fine growth of large white pine that had been sought out by the early lumbermen.

Mast Logs from the Swift River

The Swift River flows easterly into the Saco River at Conway, after flowing across the northern portion of the town of Albany, and has its source near what is now known as Kancamagus Pass. In this twenty-mile long valley and along the lower mountain slopes south of the river, the Saco River loggers originally found some magnificent stands of large white pine well suited for harvest as ship mast logs for the coastal ship builders.

In 1668 the provincial government of Massachusetts had enacted the English broad arrow policy, reserving any pine measuring at least two feet in diameter at a point one yard above the ground for exclusive use as Royal ship masts. A similar law was passed in the area known as New Hampshire in 1708, and many mast logs were harvested along the rivers in lower New Hampshire for the boat-building industry.

Felling a mast tree required exceptional care, lest the tree break or split. A bed would often be prepared by the loggers to cushion the fall, unless logging in deep snow. The length of the mast log cut from the tree would depend on the tree size, usually calculated as a yard in length for each inch in diameter at the butt end of the log. Thus, a log 24 inches in diameter on the butt end would be about 72 feet in length. There are accounts of mast logs as large as 110 feet in length and two feet in diameter on the small end.

Moving the huge log down to the nearest river was quite a task. At times the distance could be considerable, even up and over hills, to a stream large enough to float the large pine log the long distance to the shipyards. A vehicle commonly used was a pair of high-wheeled axles to which the log was chained high up in the air on the underside of the axles. Anywhere from sixteen to forty yoke of oxen were hitched onto the front end, with two additional yoke placed on each side between the fore and hind set of high wheels.

It didn't take long, of course, before suitable large mast trees would become depleted in any given area. As the supply dwindled in lower New Hampshire the loggers would move further and further north. Thus it was, then, that in the late 1700s the timber lookers became aware of a resource of large white pine in the Swift River valley, and loggers were sent into the area.

Removing the mast logs presented a challenge because there was no road built up along the Swift River in the eighteenth century; the town road was not laid out until 1837. So those early mast loggers cut their own road out of the Swift River country to the nearest river suitable for log driving. Starting at an intervale on the Swift River that later became known as Passaconaway, the mast road went on an upgrade in a southerly direction to pass between Mt. Passaconaway and Mt. Paugus and thence down through the Wonalancet area. The mast logs were probably rolled into the Ossipee River for the float trip down into the Saco River.

About the time that a town road was later established along the Swift River

This 1918 photo of virgin spruce on the summit of Mt. Paugus, taken at the edge of a cutting operation, shows the smaller tree size found at higher elevations.
U.S. Forest Service photo

U.S. Forest Service District Ranger Verland Ohlson was awed by this large white pine that had been marked for harvest as a mast log but was never cut. This photo was taken in 1962 on the Rob Brook timber sale; the tree was not cut down.
U.S. Forest Service

to accommodate the scattered settlers along the valley, especially at Passaconaway, other loggers moved in to harvest more of the softwood timber and to hopefully drive the logs down the Swift River. But they found the rocky and crooked Swift River to be quite uncooperative. Sluiceways and dams were built and considerable blasting was done on the rocky obstructions, but the Swift River was not to be tamed. The river-driving attempts lasted only a few short years, ending sometime in the 1840s.

Those early loggers didn't remove all of the mast-size white pine, however. When the railroad loggers invaded the Swift River valley at the beginning of the twentieth century, they discovered there were still a number of large old-growth white pine to be harvested. One of the loggers later recalled how a single pine tree once made up an entire trainload.

State Disposes of Mountain Timberland

The small sawmills that were established along the upper Saco River and along the Swift River in the mid-1800s made only a small dent in the abundant timber supply along the mountain ridges. Actually, the large expanses of mountain timberland didn't belong in local ownership anyhow. Wealthy individuals and corporations from out of state had been able to obtain title to a large portion of the White Mountains timber resource and were not making it available.

At one time well back in history, the state of New Hampshire owned all of the mountain land. Then in 1810 the state began an effort to dispose of the timberland and, especially from about 1830 onward, the policy was to sell the vast forested areas quickly and cheaply. A Mr. Willey of Conway was appointed as a local land commissioner in 1831 and given a six percent commission on all land sales he arranged. As an example of land values at the time, Willey sold a 33,941-acre parcel for $1,023 and another 10,000-acre tract for $300, or 3 cents per acre.

This liquidation policy by the state opened the door for the out-of-state timber industry to acquire large forested tracts along the mountain slopes. Then with many of the large ownerships it became a case of liquidating the timber wealth and later selling the cut-over land, frequently to the newly formed White Mountain National Forest. Liquidation in some cases meant the establishment of a large sawmill and possibly an accompanying mill village and a logging railroad for the duration of the timber harvest.

Land-holding companies such as the Publisher's Paper Company and the New Hampshire Land Company were able to amass large acreages throughout the White Mountains. George James, organizer of the New Hampshire Land Company in 1880, was assailed for amassing large tracts of land by means of tax sale purchases and other cheap acquisitions, and then applying a policy of "refrigeration." He would freeze out the locals from any opportunity to use the land or to purchase standing timber. George James and the New Hampshire Land Company were to have a direct involvement in the logging railroads that were soon to invade the virgin timber of the White Mountains.

However, before the railroad loggers could move into the region, it was essential for the common carriers—or main line railroads—to build into the upper Saco River valley and thus establish a link to the outside world. This

MOUNTAIN TIMBERLAND VALUES IN 1904

Land with spruce timber =	$20–30/acre
Value of remote timber land in 1830 =	$.03/acre
Land cut over for spruce but with old-growth hardwood remaining =	$2–4/acre
Land burned over =	$1–2/acre
Spruce timber (stumpage) value =	$3.75/thousand board feet
Birch and Maple timber =	$3.00/thousand board feet
Market value of spruce lumber =	$16/thousand board feet (air dried)

The dark areas show the old-growth forest still remaining in 1894 in this map of Carroll County. This map first appeared in the 1894 report of the New Hampshire Forestry Commission

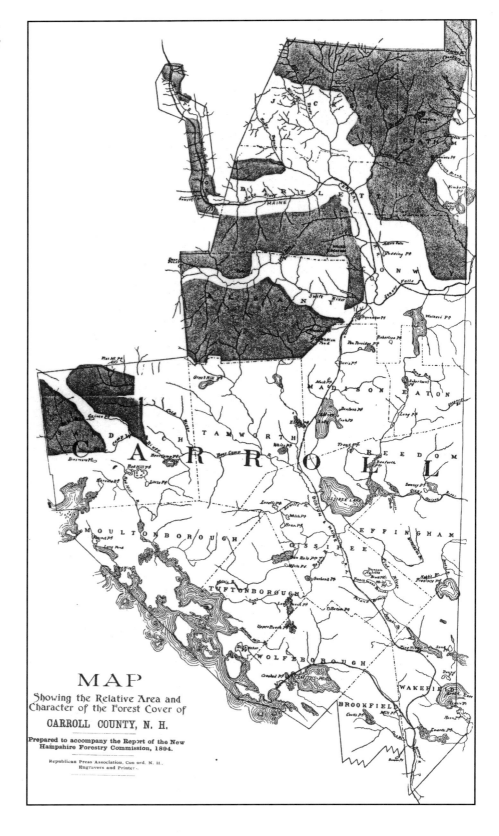

MAP

Showing the Relative Area and
Character of the Forest Cover of

CARROLL COUNTY, N. H.

Prepared to accompany the Report of the New
Hampshire Forestry Commission, 1894.

Republican Press Association, Concord, N. H.,
Engravers and Printers.

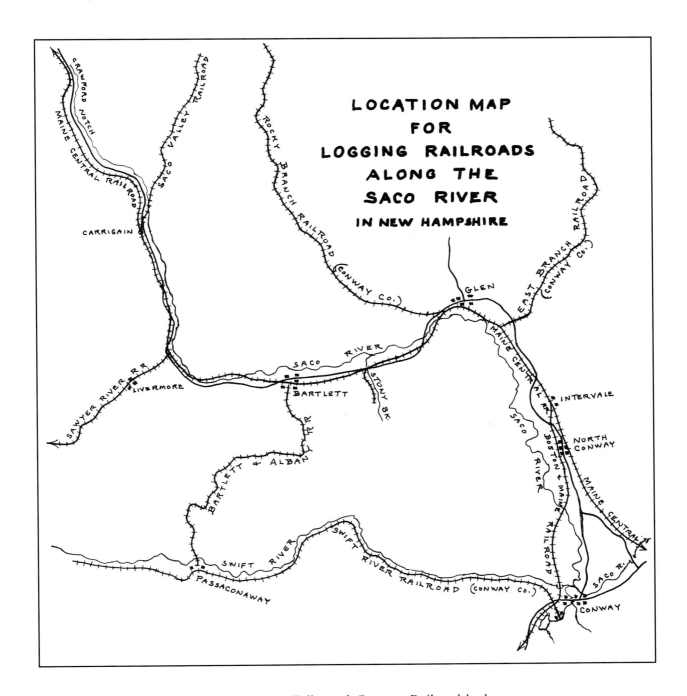

LOCATION MAP
FOR
LOGGING RAILROADS
ALONG THE
SACO RIVER
IN NEW HAMPSHIRE

occurred in 1871. The Portsmouth, Great Falls, and Conway Railroad had begun construction in 1848 and reached Conway from the south in 1871. The line was soon afterward leased to the Eastern Railroad, which in turn eventually became part of the Boston and Maine Railroad.

The Portland and Ogdensburg Railroad, building northwesterly from Portland, reached Conway in 1871, Bartlett in 1873, and Fabyan's in 1875. The P&O became part of the Maine Central Railroad in 1888. Thus the upper Saco River valley acquired two major railroad lines.

The arrival of these railroads opened an outlet to distant lumber markets,

FORESTS OF NORTHERN
NEW HAMPSHIRE IN 1904

———— ·•·• ————

200,000 acres of virgin forest remaining, 12 percent of total forest land
4,764 million board feet of softwood timber in the old-growth and
second-growth forests

and a few of the existing small sawmills in Conway and Bartlett began to flourish. In addition, new wood industries appeared along the rail line. In 1869 a spool mill was established in Conway, and in 1873 a peg mill, both of them new industries dependent on the abundant white birch resource. The spool mill would grow to be the largest thread and silk spool manufacturer in the world, employing one hundred men in the woods during the winter season cutting four thousand cords of white birch yearly.

With the new markets for lumber and other wood products, timber values took a dramatic surge upward. Values increased nine-fold over the last half of the nineteenth century, doubling between 1890 and 1900 as the big sawmills became established along New Hampshire's share of the Saco River.

Then the large sawmills, equipped with their own logging railroads, moved into the upper Saco River region starting in the late 1870s. Virgin spruce timber on the mountain slopes began to fall rapidly in the face of the loggers' onslaught, and by 1900 or shortly thereafter some watersheds were beginning to feel a shortage of available spruce timber. The railroad loggers had arrived.

The next four chapters recount the sagas of the four logging railroads that operated in the Saco River valley of New Hampshire's White Mountains. The histories cover the period 1877 to 1928, a span of fifty-one years of intense railroad logging in the White Mountains. The histories appear in the chronological order of the appearance of the company railroads.

CHAPTER TWO

Sawyer River Railroad

THE WEALTH OF New Hampshire's Saco River valley—the virgin growth of red spruce—lay tucked away among the hillsides and winding stream courses for decades after the decline of the timber resource in lower New England. Inaccessibility, conflicting land titles, and a lack of acceptance of spruce in the construction business all stood in the way of an early harvest of any consequence. That is, until the arrival of the railroads in the 1870s. Close behind came the covetous lumbermen.

From the industrial city of Lawrence, Massachusetts, the Saunders family arrived on the scene, eager to expand their lumbering opportunities and wealth into the White Mountains. They were to create the second logging railroad ever to be built in New Hampshire and, as it turned out, one that would last over fifty years and be the next-to-last logging line to cease operations. Though only nine miles in length, their rail line was able to support an active village carved into the wilderness among the mountain peaks. Known as the village of Livermore, its enchantment and seclusion became a drawing force for photographers for many years.

The Saunders brothers, Charles W. and Daniel Jr., were the progeny of Daniel Saunders, the founder of the Massachusetts City of Lawrence and its waterway system. Their interest in the lumber business and the magnet that drew them north into the White Mountains came through their marriage connections. Charles W. Saunders had married the daughter of Nicholas G. Norcross, the indisputable New England timber king, who had earned a respectable reputation as a lumberman with few equals. His name became famed on Maine's Penobscot River and the Merrimack River of Massachusetts and New Hampshire. He had dammed the Pemigewassett River and logged the old-growth white pine many years before the advent of timber baron J. E. Henry and the village of Lincoln. His large sawmill and lumber sales at Lowell, Massachusetts, had later been passed on to his sons and son-in-law Charles W. Saunders. Included in the inheritance package of timberland was an 80,000-acre tract of timberland in the White Mountains wilderness area known as the Elkins Grant. Sitting on both sides of a mountain range, it was drained by both the Saco River and the Pemigewasset River.

The other brother, Daniel Saunders Jr., had married Mary Livermore, granddaughter of Samuel Livermore, who was one of the original settlers of Holderness, New Hampshire. Daniel Saunders Jr., a Boston attorney and civic affairs leader in Lawrence, somehow obtained control of that large timberland known as the Elkins Grant from the firm of Norcross, Saunders and Company in 1862. Then a 75,000-acre township was formed from the Elkins Grant and named Livermore (for the family name of Daniel Saunders' wife) by the New Hampshire Legislature in 1876. This was not the first honor for Samuel Livermore; he previously had Livermore Falls and Mt. Livermore named after his pioneer efforts. A sawmill industry was soon to be established within this new town of Livermore, and Daniel Jr. was to become the principal in management, especially after the death of Charles W. in 1891. Eventually, Daniel Jr.'s son, Charles Gurley Saunders, was to join his father in management of the family enterprise.

These developments of the 1870s resulted in the entry of the Saunders family into the virgin forests of New Hampshire, where they were eager to tap into the green timber wealth. Family homes and law firms continued to be maintained in Massachusetts, but attractive and spacious residences were established at the new company village of Livermore, which the Saunders family was to build within their large forest holding. A sawmill industry was formed that lasted for over fifty years, although not with the blessing of the neighboring owners of other large forest tracts. Poorly defined property boundaries and the insidious acts of adjoining lumbermen to grab more timberland were to create at times a nightmare of litigation. However, the Saunders family lumber business was to outlast the existence of all of the neighboring timber barons.

The first mention of any Saunders family involvement in the upper Saco River area was in connection with an 1874 charter given for a Swift River Railroad; Daniel Saunders was one of the incorporators. Apparently a railroad up the Swift River from Conway was considered as an access route to the large Livermore property. But the charter was never acted upon, and it was left for the Conway Company to activate a similar charter about 30 years later.

The first meaningful move by the Saunders brothers was the incorporation of the Grafton County Lumber Company on July 7, 1874, followed by the selection of a sawmill site on the Sawyer River about a mile-and-a-half westerly from the junction of the Sawyer River with the Saco River. The site was to become known as the village of Livermore.

In 1875 the Portland and Ogdensburg Railroad completed their costly railroad construction up through Crawford Notch to Fabyan's, having opened the line to Sawyer's River and Bemis in August of 1874. Construction of the new sawmill at Livermore village began in 1875. But no sooner had the newly completed mill begun to operate in 1876 than it met a demise quite common to sawmills; it burned down. A second mill immediately arose from the ashes and was operational by 1877.

Daniel Saunders Sr.

An early view of a Portland & Ogdensburg freight train in the upper Saco River valley. Photo courtesy of Peter Crane

The sawmill at Livermore built in 1876 after the original mill had burned. Photo courtesy of Peter Crane

The crew of the second sawmill poses during a work break. This mill burned to the ground on October 28, 1918.

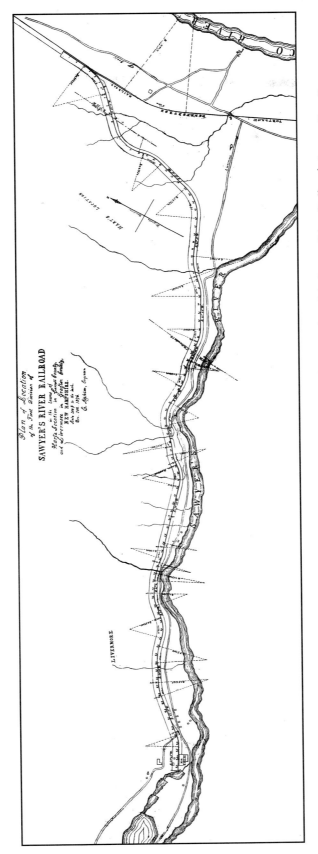

The plan prepared by surveyor E. Appleton in 1876 after completing the location survey for the initial construction of the Sawyer River Railroad. Courtesy Peter Crane

The track of the Sawyer River Railroad approaches the village of Livermore at an elevation above the row of workers' residences.
Photo courtesy of Peter Crane

The town of Livermore became incorporated in 1876 with crudely defined boundaries that had no consideration for differing mountain ranges or watershed drainages. The new 75,000-acre town contained about 30,000 acres in the Saco River watershed (via the Sawyer River), and a lofty 45,000 acres westerly over the mountain in the Pemigewasset River drainage, plus a little more land in the Mad River and Swift River watersheds. This division of property ownership irrespective of watershed boundaries was to cause the Saunders family severe headaches in the years just ahead. The village of Livermore, meanwhile, grew rapidly in its first years of existence; by 1878 the population had grown to forty-five residents.

A railroad was definitely in the plans of Daniel and Charles W. Saunders. In 1875 they had obtained a charter for the Sawyer River Railroad, empowering the builders to locate as far west as the height of land between the Pemigewasset and Sawyer Rivers. Then in December 1876, surveyor E. Appleton laid out the course for the 1.8-mile track from the Livermore depot on the P&O

A Sawyer River locomotive approaches the siding along the Maine Central track at the depot. This photo was taken prior to 1888, because the small depot is lettered "Livermore."

to the new village location to be known as Livermore. The following spring, 56-pound iron rail was laid on this segment as the initial construction began for the Sawyer River Railroad.

The small station built on the Portland & Ogdensburg at the junction point for the Sawyer River Railroad was originally known as Livermore, and then changed to Sawyer River in September 1888. There were three different station buildings over the years. In 1882 the P&O scheduled one stop daily in each direction at Livermore, a westbound mixed freight (passenger and freight cars), and an eastbound passenger train. Both were scheduled to arrive at Livermore at 6:40 P.M., where they were held for a train meet. Livermore was also listed as a flag stop for other trains passing through.

By the year 1880 there were at least twenty simple dwellings in Livermore village supporting a population exceeding one hundred. The new school already had twenty-eight pupils requiring two teachers at a salary of $26 per month. The sawmill, rebuilt new in 1877 after the fire, was not as large as some mills of that era but was still capable of sawing upwards of ten million board feet annually. The Grafton County Lumber Company was apparently prospering under the management of sawmill and company store manager William G. Hull. Most of the mill's lumber sales were handled out of the company's Boston office. By this early date, however, Daniel Saunders Jr. apparently wanted out of the enterprise, and in March 1880 he conveyed all of his rights to his son, Charles G.

Property Boundary Disputes

The Saunders family had barely made their presence known in the area before it became obvious that matters were not going to be peaceful and orderly out in the vast untouched timberlands that the sawmill was to depend upon for its existence. Contentions commenced in 1875 with a vigorous posturing

The original powerhouse that later burned down can be seen in the center of this early view of Livermore village.
Courtesy of Peter Crane

for land ownership limits. Disagreements over property boundaries were to become quite heated over the ensuing years, with lawsuits keeping the family's attorneys busy for several decades. More than one land dispute, in fact, was to require a Supreme Court decision to bring peace among the embittered land barons.

The Saunders family's trials and tribulations over ownership boundaries were not at all unusual among the timber barons during this era, and a glance at how the timber tracts were acquired explains much of it. Through the mid-1800s the state of New Hampshire had embarked on a policy of selling off as much of the White Mountains wilderness for which they could find buyers. Sales to the private owners consisted of large, poorly defined chunks of land. The price was small, and the land surveys were meager. Adjoining owners laid down their own boundary lines, whether established upon fact or otherwise, and the area between the two disputed property lines often contained some valuable spruce timber.

That was the case when a neighboring timberland owner and sawmiller, the Bartlett Land and Lumber Company, disputed the location of the east line of the Saunderses' 80,000-acre Elkins Grant. A lawsuit was filed in federal court in November 1875, and the dispute went all the way to the U.S. Supreme Court before a decision came forth in 1881. The decision favored the position of the Saunders family and fixed their boundary adjoining Hart's Location, Bartlett, and Albany, a property line that yet remains as part of the county line between Grafton and Carroll Counties. In 1897 the New Hampshire Legislature formally established this town line between the towns of Bartlett and Livermore.

The south boundaries of the town of Livermore became the next thorn in the side for Charles G. Saunders. That boundary, which adjoined the town of Waterville, had previously been contested by a prior owner in the 1880s, and when Saunders bought the area in 1895 from George B. James he soon discovered that he'd purchased a new headache. The disputed land was a long, narrow, 5,000-acre strip between the towns of Livermore and Waterville which ran through some prime spruce timber and which had earlier been deemed by court action to belong to the property that Saunders had later purchased.

Boundary lines were ill-defined, however—possibly conveniently so—and when the Conway Company purchased the adjoining timberland, they sent their loggers into that former disputed area. At various times from December 1906 to August 1909 the Conway Company removed timber that Saunders considered to be his. Legal action taken in December 1908 noted that the Conway Company had already cut eight million board feet of timber and two thousand cords of wood on the Saunders property. The suit sought a total of $250,000 and the sheriff attached over eight million board feet of Conway Company logs under orders of the court. Eventually, in 1913, the court handed down a decision that was again favorable to the Saunders family's position of ownership.

Probably the most bitter and hotly contested of the boundary disputes occurred near the turn of the century along the west line of the original Saunders family land purchase, the Elkins Grant. Involved in the dispute was a

The line of homes for workers with families was known as Railroad Row. The demeanor of the men suggests it was mid-day on a Sunday.

timber baron as tough as they come, James E. Henry, plus a greedy land buyer who was often in the middle of land controversies, George B. James.

The tales and deeds of George James are enough in themselves to form a scandalous activity chapter in the forest history of the White Mountains. Based in Boston, James began to buy up large tracts of prime timberland in the latter part of the nineteenth century. His New Hampshire Land Company was formed in 1880, and hundreds of thousands of acres passed through the hands of George James.

James never established a sawmill industry himself and apparently didn't personally set up a logging business either. But he was notorious for his land-grabbing activities and greedy exploitations of the timber resource. Historian Francis Belcher referred to him as "the will-of-the-wisp friend of both the lumberman and the conservationist." He gave lectures and published articles on the need for the preservation of the White Mountain forests; at the same time he did his utmost as land agent to put big land tracts into the hands of large-scale lumber operators for timber removal.

The presence of George James had a direct effect on the life of Charles G. Saunders in the late 1880s, eventually precipitating the Saunders family's border war with James E. Henry. Whether or not business was then prosperous for Charles G. Saunders at the Livermore sawmill is not known, but for some reason Saunders decided to sell the mill and timberland in 1886. In April he drew up an agreement with George James and the New Hampshire Land Company to sell James his land and buildings in Grafton County for $100,000. The mortgage given back to Saunders was to cover at least seventy thousand acres of timberland.

The Sawyer River Railroad would remain under the control of Charles Saunders during the mortgaged period, charging James only five cents per thousand board feet for lumber carried out to the Maine Central depot. When the mortgage was released, James was to receive all interest in the railroad as well as the charter and stock of Grafton County Lumber Company. Apparently there had already been some legal difficulties between Saunders and James, because one of the stipulations in the agreement stated that upon final execution of the deed all court cases between the two parties would be settled with judgment in favor of the defendants (Grafton County Lumber Company and Charles G. Saunders).

Deeds were passed the following year and George James appears to have made an effort at operating the Livermore mill. But matters did not work out well between the two timber barons. Payments on the mortgage fell behind to the point where Charles Saunders foreclosed and took possession without notice in August of 1890. Saunders' action was legally contested by James in a complaint filed the next year, with James claiming that Saunders took advantage of the financially embarrassed condition that he was experiencing and fraudulently compelled the transfer of titles. The challenge went to court in November 1891; this time it was George James who lost out to Saunders.

In the midst of the Saunders–James legal wrangle, James E. Henry received title to that portion of the Town of Livermore which was on the west side of the mountain range and was thus drained by the Pemigewasset River. It involved a maze of complicated deeds, but it made sense because that portion of Livermore—about forty-five thousand acres—was not accessible to Saunders' railroad. Henry's purchase of the land set the stage for the next boundary dispute.

The property line between the new Henry tract and Charles G. Saunders' tract had been stated in the deeds as the height-of-land between the Pemigewasset River drainage on the west side and the Saco River drainage on the east. Such a definition is probably sufficient on the upper mountain slopes, but in the basin and saddles between the mountains, such a definition can be vague with a property line difficult to physically locate. And it was in these pockets, of course, that the valuable timber was located and that trouble ensued.

Cutting crews from both sides continually cut over into one another's drainage, creating hard feelings between the timber owners. At one point Henry went so far as to send the sheriff up to the ridgetop to arrest Saunders' entire cutting crew, which was then taken to Lincoln and locked up in the local jail. Charles G. Saunders' counsel, George F. Morris, had to arrange for bail so that the loggers could be freed.

In an effort to settle the timber dispute, a judge hearing the case ordered that an estimate be made to determine the volume of timber trespass cut by each party. Attorney George Morris was representing Saunders' interest in the investigation, and he reported that a week was spent along the ridges counting the stumps of trees cut by either party on the wrong side of the height of land. The investigators found that Henry's trespass far exceeded that committed by Saunders' loggers, especially in the valley between Mts. Huntington and Hancock, where an exceptional stand of spruce timber was growing. The case never came to trial, however; instead, Henry reluctantly agreed to pay a large cash settlement. George Morris later assisted surveyor Ray T. Gile as he established and marked a property boundary line along the height-of-land, a task which covered a length of 60 miles and required parts of two years to complete.

The bad feelings between Charles G. Saunders and J. E. Henry had existed even before the trespass dispute, and this litigation only served to make matters much worse. One story, recorded many years ago, claims that Henry established a few men of voting age as residents in some of his logging camps located within the then-existing town of Livermore on the Pemigewasset side of the mountain ridge. His intention was to have enough town residents from his camp attend the Livermore town meeting and attempt to assume local political control. Henry's hope was that this would lead to a reduction in the high taxes being assessed upon his horses, camps and equipment.

As the annual town meeting was convened at the Livermore store—with eighteen residents, all Saunders employees, in attendance—a boy fishing along the Sawyer River spotted Henry's men walking briskly down a logging road, headed for the advertised meeting. The boy sped back into town and informed those at town meeting of the impending arrival of Henry's men. Hearing this, the town meeting was immediately adjourned, minutes before the Henry group's arrival.

The Saunders–Henry boundary war finally came to an end in 1901 with a legislative act authorizing a division of the Town of Livermore. In accordance with the act, the land on the east side of the mountain range, in the Pemigewasset drainage, was annexed to the Town of Lincoln, with the transfer completed in 1908.

Sawyer River Railroad

As previously related, the first segment of the railroad was laid down in 1877 from the Sawyer River depot on the Maine Central to the sawmill village of Livermore. As was customary for the builders of logging railroads, second-hand rail and other track equipment was leased from one of the large railroads. Three miles of rail were initially obtained from the Eastern Railroad (later the B&M) and further supplemented in 1880 by an extended agreement for another five miles of rail, switches and frogs.

The railroad was built westerly from the mill up into the headwaters of the Sawyer River, as well as an extended branch southerly into the Swift River drainage terminating on the Swift River, just north of Lily Pond. Above Camp 6, the rails crossed the Swift River several times. The total length of the main line was about nine miles, but sidings and yard trackage pushed the total up to about ten miles of rail.

In the later years of new line construction, more rail was needed, so in 1907 another rail shipment arrived from the Boston and Maine Railroad (successor to the Eastern Railroad). The B&M renegotiated an increase in the rental figure, but the Saunderses objected to the new contract rental fee, reminding the B&M on more than one occasion that Saunders could confine their outgoing lumber traffic to the Maine Central if there was no agreement on terms. B&M President James H. Hustis is reported by Francis Belcher as having written an internal management memo stating: "In negotiating this contract the value of the Sawyer River Lumber Company business to the Boston and Maine should be fully understood by the officer conducting the negotiations." The annual track rental fee is reported to have been set at three percent of the value of the rail, which was valued at $25 per ton.

Logging railroads were not built to accommodate fast traffic, as evidenced by this 1916 photograph of the Sawyer River Railroad line.

The Sawyer River Railroad was a single-locomotive operation. For most of the life of the pike, the locomotive was a 30-ton wood-burning 0-4-0 purchased new from the Portland Company in November of 1876 and named the *C. W. Saunders*. The engine had many years of service, but it had a difficult time staying on the track in later years. Probably that was to be expected after 44 years of rough service on a logging line.

By 1920 the *C. W. Saunders* had suffered its last excursion off the rails when it rambled down into the Sawyer River. Engine parts were salvaged, but the boiler remained in the riverbed for many years. As a replacement, the company bought a small 25-ton 2-4-2 Baldwin from the Conway Company that had been built back in 1886 for James E. Henry. The little saddletank had already struggled through four owners and thirty-four years of logging duties, but it managed a few more short years of duty for Saunders, who had it repaired and painted at the Bartlett engine house. The saddletank became a familiar sight at Sawyer River depot on the Maine Central, where it would await the northbound afternoon train to pick up mail and passengers en route to Livermore village.

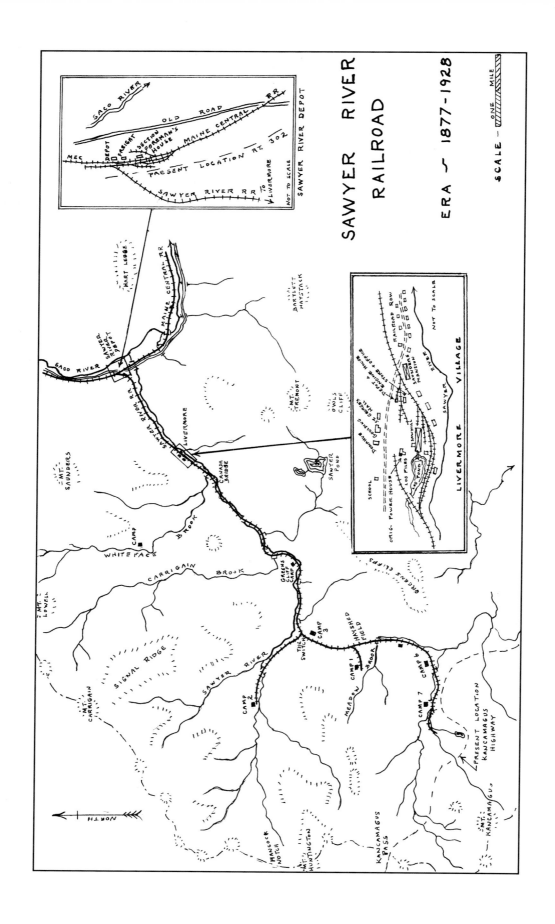

SAWYER RIVER RAILROAD

ERA ~ 1877-1928

SCALE — ONE MILE

For rolling stock, the Sawyer River Railroad used individual log trucks consisting of a log bunk mounted on top of a single truck; the couplers were link-and-pin. Thirty-five new log trucks were purchased from the Portland Company in 1876, with an additional eighteen identical trucks added in 1895. The log trucks took a beating in the woods and replacements were frequent. In 1916 about eighteen surplus trucks—most of which had been built at the Waterville, Maine, shops—were obtained from the Maine Central. The *Northwestern Lumberman* reported that the company also had sixteen log cars built by the Laconia Car Company.

The 30-ton C. W. Saunders, *built by Portland Company in 1876, saw its entire life of service on the Sawyer River Railroad.*

That's not the engineer posing on the nose of the C. W. Saunders *in July 1910.*

The designation "No. 1" was restored to the old Baldwin saddletank when it began duty on the Sawyer River Railroad in 1920. This photograph was taken at the MEC depot, where a boxcar was being delivered.

The Baldwin at work next to the log pond. The Livermore schoolhouse can be seen in the background.

A wood-framed log truck with a load of fine spruce logs. Photo courtesy of Ed Clark

The link-and-pin coupling system.

Pictured here is a four-wheel flat car used to carry supplies. Brakes were applied by a hand-tightened brake beam pressing against the wheels, as with the log cars.

27

The Saunderses would not provide a passenger car of any type on the Sawyer River Railroad. Here, fifteen well-dressed folks have just arrived at the Sawyer River depot and are loaded, baggage and all, onto the tender for the transport into Livermore village.

The average load per car was four thousand board feet of spruce, but this declined somewhat in later years as the logs became much smaller. The railroad was hauling eight to ten million board feet annually.

The only supply cars normally used to carry freight and passengers into the Livermore village were two 4-wheel flatcars built by the Portland Company in 1877. They were frequently wrecked and then rebuilt at Livermore. Foreign flats and boxcars were also brought in for loading at the sawmill. Snow was plowed by a homemade plow mounted on a log truck. A large Portland Company wedge plow was on the site for a few years but presented a problem because the only turnaround was the wye at the Maine Central interchange.

The C. W. Saunders appears to have been still fairly new when photographed here performing switching duties.

Charles Saunders would not accept a mail contract for delivery to Livermore because he did not want the Sawyer River Railroad to be responsible for making the required daily trip to the MEC junction with their only locomotive. He also would not put a passenger car of any type on his railroad.

Among the Sawyer River locomotive engineers were James Lane (who later worked for Conway Company), Rob Bennet, Roy Emery, and Edward Sinclair of Bartlett, possibly the last engineer on the operation. John Monahan, a rugged Irishman from Leeds, Quebec, worked many years at Livermore as foreman on the railroad and camp boss on the log jobs. His brother, James, was also a logging camp foreman.

Accidents on the Sawyer River Railroad were all too frequent. A few of the grades on the woods line were a little too much for the *C. W. Saunders* to hold back with a full load. There was one curve on a downgrade where the locomotive took off into the woods on at least three different occasions. The train would sometimes be late leaving Livermore to make connections with the Maine Central, with the occasional result that careless haste meant derailments.

Maine Central's large steam crane was not able to travel on the Sawyer River tracks to do any salvage work on the frequent wrecks; the light rails and weak bridges couldn't support the machine. The locomotive and cars had to be put back on the tracks with a hand derrick. While the *C. W. Saunders* underwent its frequent repairs, the Maine Central would send up a 4-4-0 shifter from the Bartlett yard to help out with the log hauls.

The C. W. Saunders rests in the woods after one of its unplanned excursions off the track.

The boiler is still steaming after an accident that appears to have resulted from an early springtime washout or track heave.

One of the tender trucks ended up on top of the cab during this mishap.

With the tender eventually wrecked, the company shop built a temporary fuel box on a log truck which soon proved to be too small. This resulted from an earlier wreck as evidenced by the original cab still intact.

What could fascinate a young fella more than a spectacular wreck. With a Maine Central box car in tow, the accident apparently occurred on the track from Livermore out to the MEC depot.

THE SAGA OF THE WANDERING
C. W. SAUNDERS

The little locomotive named the *C. W. Saunders* was not the ideal style of locomotive for use on the crooked, rough trackage of a logging railroad. With the absence of any smaller lead and trailing wheels, the 48-inch drivers frequently strayed from the rails. According to one report, the *C. W. Saunders* had 33 different accidents and wrecks during the engine's 44-year lifetime.

The vulnerable cab was occasionally wrecked beyond repair, and there were at least two or three wooden replacement cabs created at the Livermore shop. The tenders took a destructive beating during the mishaps; the locomotive is known to have had at least three different tenders. The photos of the wrecks seem to indicate many of the accidents occurred during the later years of operation.

In 1920 the *C. W. Saunders* suffered its last excursion off the rails, straying into the Sawyer River. For many years afterward the locomotive boiler sat on the riverbed and then was later seen resting at the Maine Central's Sawyer River station.

The original cab disappeared after a later excursion off the track, but the crew had to continue operations with its only locomotive while the shop fashioned a replacement cab. Fortunately, the weather was not bitter cold.

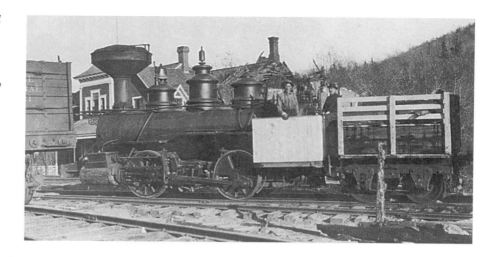

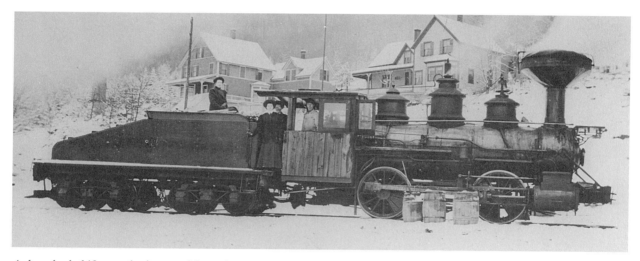

A slant-back shifter tender borrowed from the Maine Central became a temporary replacement. The cab has been rebuilt. In the background are the Goulding House (left) and St. George's Hall.

The slant-back over the tender's water tank made a convenient, if not comfortable, seat for passengers to ride to the depot. Note that the locomotive had received its name again, this time with a different lettering style.

The boiler of the C. W. Saunders was brought out to a siding at the MEC depot a few years after the 1920 wreck, which was the final mishap.

It was not unusual to hear reports about the entire train crew being told to jump pending a disaster. There was one reported incident when a canvasser named Gallaher was riding in the locomotive cab and was told to jump when the engineer couldn't hold back the heavy load. Gallaher leaped, landed in the deep snow, but rolled back down the steep bank and under the wheels. End of story unknown.

Rob Bennet, locomotive engineer for four summers, once had a harrowing experience near the sawmill. He was underneath the engine with his oil

Flatcars are loaded with lumber ready for shipment.

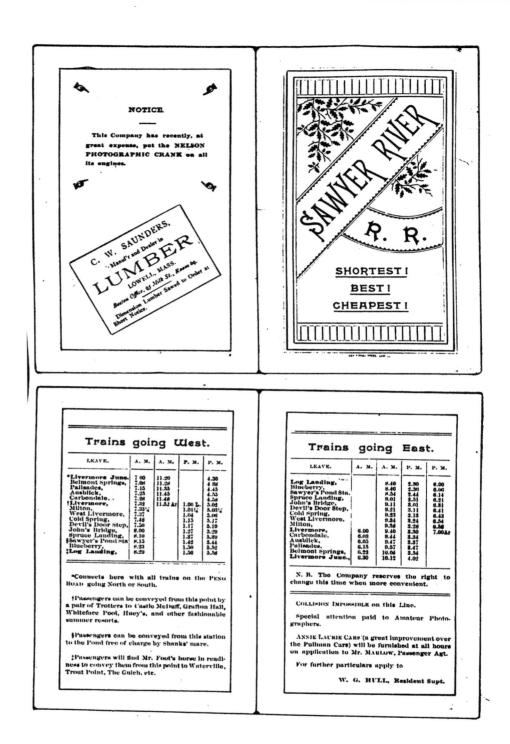

A tongue-in-cheek train schedule prepared by the manager of the Sawyer River Railroad.

can when a car back at the mill broke loose when a wheel trig came out. As the men shouted from up above, Bennet scrambled out from under, leaped onto the locomotive and started it down the hill so that the car careening toward him made only a gentle collision with the locomotive.

Brakeman Richard Whitty was not as fortunate back in 1882 when he was run over by moving cars.

Livermore Village

By the year 1890 the village population of Livermore had grown to 155, with about twenty dwellings and, of course, a boarding house for the many single employees in the mill. All structures were owned by the Saunders interests, including the company store where all residents were expected to make their purchases. Goods were cheaper on the outside, of course, and Louis Chaffee of Bartlett found a way to profit on that situation. He would park out at the entrance to the Livermore road with a wagon load of groceries and staples and wait for buyers to come out to him; all after dark, of course. William G. Hull was store manager in the early years, as well as postmaster. The post office was established at Livermore in March of 1881.

Saunders had to build a new schoolhouse after the state of New Hampshire made an official complaint about the educational facilities at Livermore. But there were never more than twenty or so pupils attending the school. A visitor once described the entire contents of the schoolhouse as a large world

The Saunders family mansion known as The Forests.

The Goulding House.

globe, a Victrola, slate blackboards, a large wood stove and well-painted seats and desks. Annie Fahey was one of the school's earlier teachers.

One of the more notable village residents was Levi Dumas, who later gained fame in the area as a builder of specialized railroad equipment for J. E. Henry's East Branch and Lincoln Railroad out of Lincoln. Born in Canada in 1857, Dumas was working as a carpenter in Livermore in 1900. His services undoubtedly proved valuable with his self-taught skills plus his ability to read and write.

Livermore's Main Street was quite muddy down along the workers' homes on Railroad Row in 1919.

The company store and freight building, seen here, also housed the company office.

The original schoolhouse at Livermore and what appears to be the entire student body.

The sawmill during the early years of the village was operating an eleven-hour day with about twenty-five employees. There were two circular saws supplemented for further breakdown of the logs by five muley saws, a band saw and a sash gang saw with eighteen blades. Lath and shingles were produced in addition to the spruce boards and dimension lumber. Five 150-horsepower boilers supplied the steam power.

The mill was not a big one, as the major sawmills tended to be during this era. During those years the mill normally operated eleven months out of the year with an annual lumber production of four million board feet. Production in 1880, however, was low for some unexplained reason; only 2.5 million

Stacks of kindling wood—cut from the sawmill edgings—and slab wood are seen in this early view of the mill area. The boxcar seen to the right is being loaded for shipment to urban areas.

Many of the logs were dumped down the bank from the railroad track above the mill pond.

The sawmill crew poses on the log slip, which carried the logs up into the mill.

board feet of lumber were sawn. Spruce logs delivered to the mill were valued at about $9.20 per thousand board feet. Wages for laborers were $1.35 per day; $1.75 for the skilled workers. William Hull was superintendent of the mill at that time.

A name fondly remembered by village residents was that of "Big Jim" Donahue, who had arrived on the scene in 1888 at age nineteen. Donahue was eventually to wear many hats: sawmill manager, town manager, postmaster,

The mill pond crew worked the logs up to the sawmill entrance.

Parked in front of the company store, the group seen here is about to leave for one of the remote logging camps along the Sawyer River line. Jim Donahue is the tall man in the rear wearing a cap. The building on the left is believed to have been the engine house.

Fred A. Lane (left) and Frank Chisholm with what appears to be the drive wheels off of the C. W. Saunders.

railroad agent, selectman, town clerk, etc. He died in 1928, about 59 years young.

The town census of 1900 showed a village population of 191 residents, which quite possibly was the peak number during the sixty-year year existence of Livermore village.

By the early 1900s the sawmill had come under different management and apparently under lease to other operators. The mill was destroyed by fire for the second time in November 1918, and operations were apparently suspended for a couple of years, or until construction of a new mill began in

Pictured here is the new Livermore sawmill built in 1920–22. This was the third mill to be constructed on the site.

1920. The new sawmill—the third one—began operations by 1922 under the name of Livermore Mills Company. The mill was valued at $45,000.

Logging Activities

After completion of the boundary line squabbles and land exchanges with adjoining landowners, Charles G. Saunders settled down with about thirty thousand acres of timberland to supply the sawmill with logs. With his conservative cutting practices, the timberland was able to furnish the needed raw material for over fifty years, unusual in that era of large, short-lived sawmills and massive clearcuts of the timber.

There were at least seven logging camps established over the years housing over 150 loggers harvesting the spruce in the Sawyer River valley. Many of the woods and mill workers were obtained through an employment office in

Camp No. 2 with the blacksmith shop on the left, the horse barn, and the combined bunkhouse and cook shack. The Saunders camps were typically covered on the outside with tar paper.

Camp No. 3 during what appears to be a summertime lull in activity. The log loading skidways are on the right.

A corduroyed log sled road built above Camp 6.

Massachusetts, and many of these itinerant workers were not of the best character. Some didn't stay for long; a few even attempted to flee before repaying their debts in clothing and other supplies. This was a continuing problem, which prompted Charles G. Saunders to hire a man named Sidney White, whose job was to discourage the absconders. According to one written account, White once shot a man, Bidwood Blair, in the leg as he was fleeing Livermore. The case went to court at the county seat in Ossipee and Saunders ended up paying a $3,000 fine.

The loggers who stuck with it were a rugged bunch, but accidents were frequent and considered to be acceptable occupational risks. Consider a few actual examples on the Sawyer River: 1886—logger Michael Guinan is killed by a falling tree; 1895—Alphonse Thereault is crushed by logs; 1907—laborer Peter Mace is killed by a log team.

It's hard to believe that liquor would ever be allowed in the logging camps, but the determined woodsman had a way of acquiring strong drink. There was an occasion when some drunken loggers from Livermore ended up in Bartlett and broke into the home of James Nute, where they demanded some

Logs were loaded on the railroad cars by hand from elevated skidways built railside. This particular loading area had a large backup of spruce logs on the steep hillside.

In areas without a bank high enough to build a skidway, the logs were loaded with a swing boom. The logs were raised by means of a hand crank and pushed to swing the boom.

In this instance anyway, much of the railroading appears to have been done before deep snows accumulated. Photo courtesy of Peter Crane.

The railroad made a number of river crossings as it wound its way up along Sawyer River.

food. The inebriates were arrested by Constable Chesley but later broke out of jail and took off for places unknown.

Much has been made by writers of that era over the conservative cutting practices of Saunders in his spruce stands. If recorded descriptions of the Saunders cutting methods are accurate, the harvested lands would have made quite a contrast with the barren clearcuts so common at that time. Saunders was reported to have logged some of his land as many as three different times, making only partial cuts in each instance.

The first time through, only the spruce and other softwoods larger than fourteen inches in diameter at the stump height, plus a mixture of hard-woods, were cut. For a virgin stand that would still be a fairly heavy cut. A few years later, possibly twenty or more, the land was logged again, this time down to a ten-inch stump diameter. And again, a third cut was said to be made in some areas, this time down to a seven-inch stump diameter. There is no question but what such a conservative cutting practice would lessen the profusion of dry slash left after a heavy cutting. Thus it is well to note that the Sawyer River country never suffered a forest fire of any significance.

However, diameter-limit cuttings are not the same as selective cuttings, which will account for factors such as tree spacing and site conditions. At best, the Saunderses' diameter-limit cuts, commendable as they were for the era,

There is little left standing in this clearcut above Camp 7. An uncut stand of old-growth spruce can be seen in the background.

The only growth left on this hillside by the Charles G. Saunders logging crews was an occasional spruce and some small hardwood. Note the log sled road following the contour. Photo courtesy of Peter Crane

had extended the company's harvesting on the thirty thousand acres to last for a few extra years. The ingrowths during the intervening periods between cuts would add to the next cut, but not significantly. The sawmill required only about four million board feet annually—not a large volume—and no pulpwood was cut. Thus, the demand for logs was not great. But the final cut down to a seven-inch stump is a heavy cut, and there couldn't have been much at all left on the land after that. For practical purposes, the final harvest left a clearcut, which was no different than what his contemporaries were leaving behind elsewhere in the forests of northern New England. The mill must have been sawing a preponderance of small logs in the 1920s, with the large trees having been removed years before.

Despite years of lumbering in the area, one patch of eight to ten million

A number of spruce butt logs from small trees can be seen in this trainload coming out in 1906, evidence that the logging was not confined to large trees only.

board feet of virgin timber—along the eastern slopes of Mt. Kancamagus and Mt. Huntington at the head end of the Swift River—remained uncut in 1920. The Saunders Estate decided to harvest the area, but by then had abandoned their partial-cut policy, and they clearcut the entire patch. They were discouraged by the state's taxation policy but no doubt had in mind that the days of operation in Sawyer River were now numbered.

Last Years

With the 1918 death of Charles G. Saunders at age 70, there were no longer any of the Saunders men living to control operations. Ownership continued in the estate primarily by the three sisters of Charles G., who lived at Livermore for a portion of the year. Clinton Nash represented the Saunders Estate.

After the sawmill burned in 1918, it was rebuilt and operating two years later by interests other than the Saunders heirs. At that time the future outlook for Livermore seemed to take an upturn. The village population grew to ninety-eight from a low of sixty-four back in 1910. A new schoolhouse was built in 1923. But disaster struck in the fall of 1927; the destructive floods that swept across northern New England filled the Sawyer River with a devastating volume of rushing water. The Sawyer River Railroad, which followed the stream courses, was damaged beyond feasible repair. Only four miles remained usable in the flood's aftermath.

Regular rail operations on the Sawyer River line ceased and the mill closed permanently in 1928. Realizing there was no future for the village, Clinton Nash approached the U.S. Forest Service about buying the Saunders family's land. The federal government, which had initially contacted the Saunders family about selling the land ten years earlier (after the Weeks Act of 1911 had established the National Forest system in the Eastern United States),

The sawmill built in 1920 to replace the mill that burned in 1918 operated only until 1928, when the entire Sawyer River operation permanently closed down.

expressed interest once again in purchasing the land. But as was the case a decade earlier, the price the government was willing to pay was not attractive enough for Nash to accept.

In the meantime, the village continued to survive, but barely so. Livermore's population slid to twenty-three people by 1930, with the local post office closing in 1931 and the school in 1935. The remaining rails on the Sawyer River Railroad were also pulled in 1935. In 1934 the three Saunders sisters signed an option to sell the timberland to the U.S. Forest Service, and the deal was completed in 1937. The federal government purchased the 29,900 acres for about $9 per acre, the exception being some inholdings in Livermore village. This was below what Nash had hoped to get for the land, as he had been holding out for $12 per acre with the claim that there were 25 to 30 million board feet of merchantable timber still standing in the Nancy Brook area.

It was during the era of Franklin Roosevelt's Civilian Conservation Corps (CCC) that crews began dismantling what was left of Livermore village, and in 1936 the CCC workers discovered the little Baldwin 2-4-2 locomotive still stashed away in a shed. The locomotive was towed down to the Maine Central's Sawyer River depot, where it sat on a siding for quite some time. According to some sources, the Baldwin was scrapped at that spot; other reports say it was sold. Whatever its final disposition, the disappearance of the Baldwin engine from Sawyer River marked the final chapter in a storied life of forty-two years of railroad logging on at least five different logging railroad lines. No wonder some referred to the locomotive as the "old lady of the mountains."

Most of the railroad bed was built close to the Sawyer River bed and was vulnerable to damage by high water. Mt. Carrigain is visible in the background.

The Baldwin saddletank sat at the siding by the former Maine Central Sawyer River depot for a few months in about 1936. It had been dragged down there by CCC workers.

As for Livermore village, it, too, died a slow death. The town census of 1940 showed just four residents still living at the inholding surrounded by National Forest property. Then it all came to an unnoticed end in 1949 when Joe Platt, the last village resident, moved out of town. Two years later, the town of Livermore was officially dissolved by an act of the state legislature and thus became an unincorporated township within the White Mountain National Forest. Meanwhile, Edith Saunders, the last of the three sisters and the last of the Saunders family, died at age 84.

BARTLETT AND ALBANY RAILROAD

——◆◆◆——

Dates: 1887–1893
Owner: Bartlett Land and Lumber Company
Products hauled: Softwood and hardwood sawlogs, hemlock bark
Length: 13 miles

Equipment

Locomotive: *Albany*, 2-6-0, CN 554
Built 1887 by Portland Company
Bought new, cylinders 17" × 24", wheels 50"
Disposition unknown

Cars: Log trucks, about 20 pair
Flat and freight cars
Wedge plow
Four-wheel flats

The original depot and freight shed in Bartlett is seen in this photo taken while the rail line was still the Portland & Ogdensburg Railroad.

CHAPTER THREE

The Bartlett and Albany Railroad

T HE VILLAGE OF Bartlett, New Hampshire, was once the center of railroad activity in the eastern White Mountains. During the peak of American railroading in the early 1900s, a majority of the village residents were railroad employees serving the Maine Central Railroad for the difficult climb up through Crawford Notch. During its prime, the village boasted the primary and finest passenger depot in the region, a six-stall engine house with turntable, coal storage, and the Bartlett Hotel, catering to a host of upper class vacationers.

The town's rise from obscurity began in 1873, when the newly built Portland and Ogdensburg Railroad reached the village and began train service. From Bartlett the builders worked northward into the Notch, carving a roadbed into the steep mountainside slopes for the arduous and rapid incline through Crawford Notch. The Portland and Ogdensburg Railroad served as an early gateway of commerce between the Atlantic Ocean and the Great Lakes, and soon after being built was taken over by the Maine Central Railroad in 1888.

In addition to the inspection and maintenance services for trains about to make the climb through the notch, the location provided extra pusher engines to assist on the rugged climb ahead. The elevation rose from 680 feet at Bartlett to almost 1900 feet at the head of Crawford Notch; one of the steepest rail climbs in the eastern United States. The village was a bustle of activity with over seven hundred residents at the peak in the 1920s.

At the same time that the P&O Railroad arrived in Bartlett, the seeds were sown for the formation of another railroad, this one a small logging pike known as the Bartlett and Albany Railroad. Though small in size, the

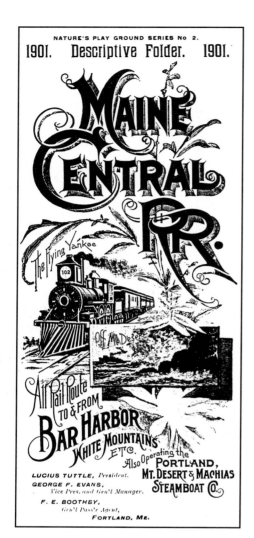

Maine Central R.R.
THE GREAT VACATION ROUTE

THROUGH TRAIN SERVICE TO THE
WHITE MOUNTAINS.

In effect Season 1900, probably same for 1901.

FROM BOSTON.

Train No.		150	160	166
Lv. Boston	Western Division......	....	8.30 am	1·15 pm
	Eastern Division......	....	9.40 "	1.30 "
Lv. North Conway..................		7.25 am	2.00 pm	5.45 "
Ar. Intervale Junction...........		7.80 "	2.13 "	6.10 "
" Glen and Jackson		7.37 "	2.21 "	6.17 "
" Bartlett....................		7.48 "	2.32 "	6.35 "
" Crawfords...................		8.40 "	3.29 "	7.25 "
" Mount Pleasant House		8.47 "	3.35 "	7.33 "
" Fabyans....................		8.50 "	3.40 "	7.37 "
Ar. Maplewood...........		9.52 am	4.17 pm	....
" Bethlehem		10.00 "	4.25 "	....
" Profile House...........		10.10 "	4.35 "	....
Ar. Twin Mountain		12.48 noon	3.50 pm	7.47 pm
Ar. Starr King (Jefferson)		1.10 pm	4.20 pm	8.10 pm
" Lancaster.....		1.24 "	4.35 "	8.25 "
" North Stratford.........			5.23 "	9.33 "
" Colebrook...............			5.50 "	10.00 "
" Quebec....................				11.45 am
Ar. Whitefield			5.23 pm	12.47 am
" Lunenburg			5.35 "	1.00 "
" St. Johnsbury...........			6.55 "	1.30 "
Ar. Montreal..................				7.35 am
" Chicago..................				10/05 "

b Third Day.

FROM PORTLAND.

Train No.	154	158	168	164	
Lv. Portland....	8.50 AM	1.05 PM	5 50 PM	8 50 PM	....
Ar. North Conway.........	10.58	3.17	8.06	10.35	
" I tervale	11.03	3.23	8.11	10.40	
" Glen and Jackson	11.10	3.30	8.18	10.47	
" Bartlett.............	11.21	3.41	8.30	10.57	
" Crawfords...........	12.18 PM	4.30	....	11.55	
" Mount Pleasant House	12.27	4.46	....	12.02	
" Fabyans............	12.30	4.50	....	12 10	
Ar. Starr King............	1.10 PM	8.10 PM	.... .	....	
" Lancaster	1.24	8.25	....	....	
" Colebr'k (Dixv'le N'ch)	2.30	10.00	....	....	
Ar. Maplewood...........	1.37 PM	5.50 PM	....	....	
" Bethlehem	1.45	6.00	....	....	
" Profile House........	1.56	7.30	....	....	
Ar. Quebec	9.15 PM	....	....	....	
Ar. Montreal.............	8.30 PM	....	....	7 35 AM	
" Chicago	a 9.45	....	....	b10.05	....

a Second day.   b Third day.

THROUGH CAR SERVICE.

No. 154, Parlor Car for Montreal, Sleeping Car for Buffalo; connecting at Fabyans with Parlor Car for Quebec, P.Q. No. 164, Sleeping Car for Montreal.

railroad's parent company played a large role in the development and growth of the once obscure hamlet of Upper Bartlett. Before long, in fact, the little hamlet was to become the prosperous railroad and sawmill village of Bartlett.

It was in the early 1870s when lumbermen Horatio and Charles Jose of Portland, Maine, began to buy up timberland in the area. In alliance with some local lumbermen, the Joses formed the Bartlett Land and Lumber Company and, in 1873, transferred their land to the company. One of their associates, C. F. Buffum, already had a steam sawmill in the village, and as soon as fresh capital became available, the sawmill was renovated for larger production. It has also been reported that there were a couple of other, smaller sawmills either in company ownership or sawing under contract. By 1875 the Bartlett Land and Lumber Company was shipping out seven million board feet annually on the P&O Railroad from the Bartlett depot.

About forty thousand acres of timberland on the slopes of Bear Mountain and Mt. Tremont and in the Swift River valley were brought into the ownership of the Bartlett Land and Lumber Company. Sledloads of logs were teamed off of the steep slopes south of the village and into the mill at Bartlett village. On the westerly side of the company ownership—along the town boundary of Bartlett and Albany—the company encountered a bitter land dispute with the neighboring landowners, as related in the chapter on the Sawyer River Railroad. The argument erupted over the obscure and unmarked

Maine Central's No. 101 was stopped on the short track between the freight house and Howard's store in this photo taken in the early years of the Maine Central Railroad at Bartlett. The main line is in the foreground, and in the rear is the line up to the big sawmill.

The large Bartlett station built by the Maine Central Railroad. Courtesy of Bartlett Library

boundaries separating the towns, and the unfriendly discussions failed to settle the dispute, which involved a large quantity of mature spruce timber. The Bartlett Land and Lumber filed a lawsuit in federal courts against Daniel and Charles W. Saunders. The case eventually went all the way to the Supreme Court before a decision was delivered in favor of the Saunderses in 1881.

As the loggers continued to strip timber off the north slopes of Bear Mountain and the other hillsides within reach of a sled with a team of rugged horses, the sawmill suffered the common tragedy of that era. In May 1888 it burned to ground level.

Business had apparently been prosperous for the owners, because the replacement was an outstanding sawmill. Three stories high and 106 feet long, the new mill was capable of sawing fifty thousand board feet of lumber daily. Adjacent to the sawmill property was another wood-using industry—the

The long tree-length spruce logs were loaded from a skidway onto the two sled for the long trip down to the mill. This type of sled consists of two separate log bunks, each mounted on its own pair of runners, one on each end of the long load.

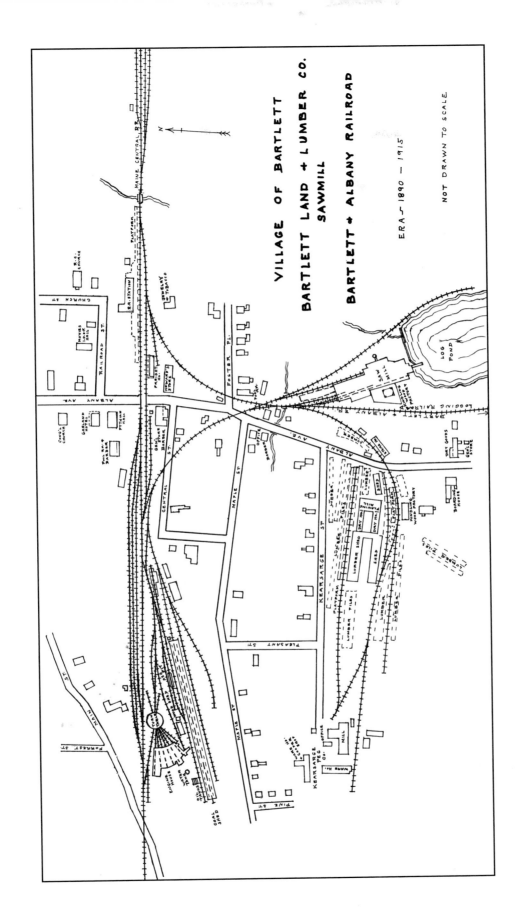

VILLAGE OF BARTLETT

BARTLETT LAND + LUMBER CO.
SAWMILL

BARTLETT + ALBANY RAILROAD

ERA — 1890 — 1915

NOT DRAWN TO SCALE.

Kearsarge Peg Company—established in 1878 by Gerry and Augustus Morgan. In 1888, Kearsarge Peg manufactured 92,000 bushels of pegs made from white birch.

The company's logging railroad became established in 1887 to reach out to the company-owned timber beyond the range of the horse loggers, but company prosperity apparently began to take a downturn after the big new sawmill was built. In 1890 the Bartlett Land and Lumber Company was sold to Otis Smith of Cambridge, Massachusetts, and Herbert W. Blanchard of Concord, Massachusetts. Included in the takeover was all of the company timberland in Carroll County, plus the mill buildings, machinery and personal property. Not included in the sale, though, was the Bartlett and Albany Railroad; the railroad had been turned over to a separate corporate ownership in 1888.

The Bartlett and Albany Railroad

The logging railroad of the Bartlett Land and Lumber Company had its beginnings in 1887. By then, most of the nearby timber had been cleared from company timberlands and a means was needed to reach further into the mountains.

A charter was granted by the State of New Hampshire in 1887 for a corporation to build a railroad from the tracks of the P&O Railroad at Bartlett in a southerly direction as far as the Swift River in Albany. The charter authorized the Bartlett and Albany Railroad to physically connect with the original Swift River Railroad (the one that had been proposed and chartered by Daniel Saunders and associates in 1874 and again in 1887, but never built). The Bartlett and Albany Railroad corporation was set up with the same leading principles as those controlling the original Bartlett Land and Lumber Company: namely, Horatio and Charles Jose. Charles Jose served as president on the railroad.

Preparation of the roadbed toward Bear Notch began in 1886. As was customary among railroad loggers, the rail was leased from one of the large railroads in the area. In September 1886 an agreement was inked with the Eastern Railroad (later part of B&M Railroad) to lease enough iron for twelve miles of railroad at an annual rental fee of three percent of the rail value. The agreed valuation was set at $28,774, providing a rental fee of about $860 for the Eastern Railroad. In return, the Bartlett and Albany had to grant a lien on their railroad right-of-way and agree to return the rail within fifteen years. The rail used was secondhand weighing 60 pounds to the yard. A further agreement for more rail was made with the Boston and Maine Railroad in 1888.

The railroad passed over the height-of-land at Bear Notch and then down into the valley of Rob Brook, culminating at the settlement known as Passa-

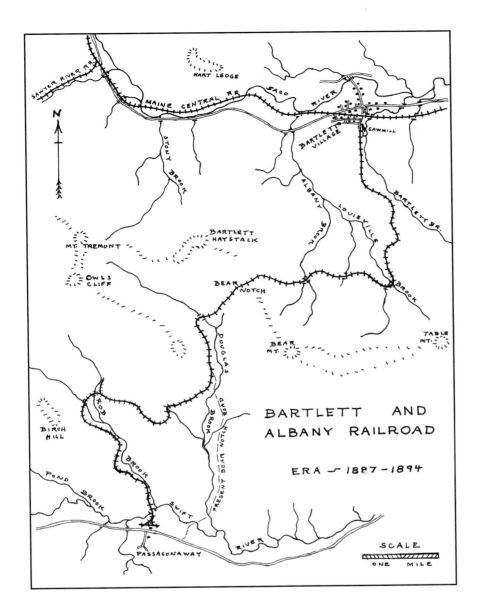

conaway on the south side of Swift River. The rails actually passed over a
mountain range and down into another valley, creating a weight limit for the
log train when headed back up and over the hill toward the Bartlett sawmill.
Most of the roadbed on the Bartlett side of Bear Notch was located where the
present-day Bear Notch highway has been built. The distance to the far end
of the line was about ten miles, but there was reported to be a total of about
thirteen miles of track at the peak of operations.

At the Passaconaway end of the line, a small railroad yard was established
on a twenty-acre piece of land purchased in 1890 from the farm of James
Mayhew. The purchase price was $400. The site was located on the south side
of the Swift River between the river and the town highway and behind the
cemetery now visible along the Kancamagus Highway. The yard included a

The Bartlett and Albany Railroad locomotive was seen parked at the Portland Company shops about 1902 after being returned to the Portland Company when the B&A had ceased operation.

Y-turnaround, a log loading deck, and an area to unload freight and load locally sawn lumber.

Operations over the entire line began in November 1887. Then the next spring, in May 1888, the Bartlett Land and Lumber Company divested itself of ownership of their new logging railroad, selling it to the corporation officers for $1,000.

The Bartlett and Albany Railroad was a one-locomotive railroad. A new mogul (2-6-0) was purchased from the Portland Company and delivered in March 1887. The coal-burning locomotive apparently had quite a decorative appearance during its early years and bore the name *Albany* on the cab.

The Maine Central Railroad continued to use the old P&O Railroad roundhouse for a number of years. In this 1893 photo the Bartlett & Albany mogul can be seen on the far right.

The Maine Central had a large six-stall engine house at Bartlett, built originally by the Portland and Ogdensburg Railroad because of the need for extra engines for use in pushing the heavy freight up through Crawford Notch. The logging locomotive of the Bartlett and Albany Railroad was kept in the engine house and was serviced by the Maine Central. During periods of locomotive repair, other engines were temporarily leased from the Maine Central. There is no report or record of a geared locomotive ever being used on the Bartlett and Albany, despite the grade over Bear Notch.

Log cars used on the Bartlett and Albany line were the traditional bunk cars or trucks, with reportedly about twenty pair once in use. In addition, there were eight or ten flat and freight cars and a wedge plow. Loading of the log cars was done by hand.

The locomotive made one trip per day, leaving Bartlett in the morning and dropping off empty trucks along the way. Supplies would be delivered to the crude logging camps en route, especially the large camp at the terminus. Loaded cars were picked up on the return and the remainder of the day was spent in shifting cars at the Bartlett mill yard.

Nobody knows how many accidents there were in the seven years of the railroad's operation, but at least one included a fatality. On August 11, 1890, road superintendent William D. Sawyer was traveling up the mountain from Bartlett with two sets of empty log trucks. Arriving at his destination for loading, he stopped on the main line. Fred Hobson and Charles Black were

A pair of log bunk trucks with a fine load of tree-length spruce. A timber or spacer was coupled between the trucks.

The old turntable in front of the roundhouse was removed by the Maine Central Railroad because it was too small to accommodate the long articulated engines used as helpers in Crawford Notch in the early 1900s. This photo was taken in 1944. Courtesy of Bartlett Library

working at the loading area and assisted in positioning the cars at the log headers. Hobson pulled the coupler pin to place one car at the first pile and jumped on the other pair of trucks to brake it upon arrival at the other loading deck, assuming the brakes were set on the first car; but they weren't. The car rolled backwards and struck Charles Black, crushing him. He had his back to the oncoming car, watching the engine to be sure it cleared the switch. Sawyer had no choice but to rush the severely injured Black down the mountain in the cab of the bouncing locomotive, load him on a Maine Central train at Bartlett, and rush him off for medical help in Portland; but he never made it. He died en route at the station in Steep Falls, Maine, close to his home.

After the logging railroad had been extended to Passaconaway on the Swift River, the railroad hauled out sawn lumber from one or more small sawmills in that area. Frank Bolles provided a description of one of the mills in his 1893 book *At the North of Bearcamp Water*. Bolles was a college professor and naturalist from Boston who had a vacation home in the area. The steam-powered circular saw mill was located a short way up along Downes Brook, with a work force of twelve laborers.

The Bartlett Land and Lumber Company's logging camps were crude affairs, sheathed with slab wood covered by tar paper. The camp on Downes Brook had a single building with a sleeping room on one end furnished with crude three-tier bunks. The inside was "dark, hot and stuffy" with a bad odor, according to the observations of Bolles, who noted also that the loggers rou-

Pictured here is the snowplow built for the Bartlett & Albany Railroad in 1890 by the Portland Company. The frame was oak, sheathed with spruce and southern pine. A similar 22-foot plow was also built for two other New Hampshire logging railroads — the East Branch & Lincoln and the Success Pond Railroads.

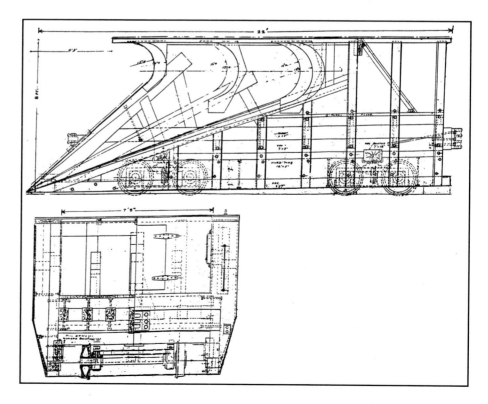

The logs were dumped from the railroad cars (seen on the left) onto the rows of logs leading into the mill pond. The sawmill is seen at the foot of the pond in this early view of the Bartlett Land & Lumber Company.
Courtesy of Bartlett Library

tinely slept with their clothes on, even though they were apt to be wet from rain or snow. The other end of the camp building contained the kitchen and dining room, with two cook stoves and three long, narrow, board tables set with tin plates and cups for thirty-five men. Bolles noted the pitchers of maple syrup, the tins with large mounds of butter, the bottles of vinegar, the plates piled high with doughnuts, and the excellent bread. Baked beans, of course, were a camp staple, along with a barrel of pork, codfish and a side of beef.

The teamsters would be roused at 4 A.M. to care for and prepare the hardworking horses for a day's toil. One teamster was noted for giving his horse a bite of chewing tobacco during a rest break, holding the plug while the horse bit it off. Wages at this time (1892) were $1 per day, plus board.

Spruce was the principal species being harvested by the lumberjacks, although the Bartlett and Albany Railroad also hauled a quantity of hemlock and hardwood logs. Any white birch harvested by the men was taken down to the Kearsarge Peg Company mill. Hemlock bark was also harvested and taken out in sheets on a flatcar for sale to the leather-tanning industry.

The logging railroad would take on riders without a charge. Bolles accepted a ride in the engine cab up to Bear Notch on a cold December day and was fascinated by the grave expression on the face of the engineer, the earnest eyes glued to the track ahead, and the firm grip on the lever. The fireman was kept busy on the upgrade pouring oil into the cups above the boiler, yanking open the fire door, shoveling in coal, ramming it down with a poker, yanking a lever to dump the ashes and then hurrying through the cycle again.

There was one occasion when some riders on a flatcar came close to not making the trip down to Bartlett alive. The locomotive broke down far from home, and the riders were exposed to the extremely cold weather. Many became seriously frozen before a Maine Central engine was able to arrive in a rescue effort, and it's been said that the company called on the services of every doctor that could be located, even one in Whitefield.

There are two different stories as to why this particular gang of men was being taken out of the woods. One version has it that there was a woodsmen's strike; the other version claims that the men in one of the camps had a drunken brawl and got evicted.

Apparently the lumber company did not prosper any better under its new owners—Otis Smith and Herbert Blanchard—who operated under the name Bartlett Lumber Company. Five years of operation had put a heavy strain on the steam system in the mill, and in 1893 a new system was installed. The Portland Company supplied three 78-inch steam boilers with 20-foot tubes, a steam drum, and a conveyor, at a cost to the company of $3,857. But the mortgages were a heavy load for Smith and Blanchard.

The logging railroad continued operating for a short time for the Smith and Blanchard ownership, but for some reason the railroad ceased to operate about 1893 or 1894. Logs were needed from an outside source, and an agreement was made with the new Saco Valley Lumber Company to accept the spruce logs brought out by their logging railroad along Dry River. The Bartlett sawmill continued to function through the 1890s but operations were dwindling.

Unsatisfied mortgages weighed heavily upon Smith and Blanchard, and in January 1894 they granted another mortgage deed, this one to lumberman Robert Osgood of Salem, Massachusetts. Osgood was the treasurer of the New Hampshire Lumber Company, which also became involved as a mortgagee of the Bartlett Lumber Company property.

By then the mortgage situation was quite complex, and things came to a head in 1905 when a Superior Court decision in the case of *Otis Smith vs.*

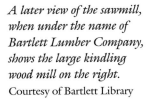

A later view of the sawmill, when under the name of Bartlett Lumber Company, shows the large kindling wood mill on the right.
Courtesy of Bartlett Library

The Bartlett and Albany Railroad tracks remained in place for a dozen or more years after the logging railroad was discontinued. This view is westerly with Owl's Cliff and Mt. Tremont in the background.

Robert Osgood and others decreed that the entire property had to be sold at a public auction. Included in the auction was a band sawmill, planing mill with a lumber dryer, a box mill, a kindling mill with a capacity of six to ten carloads of bundled wood per week, an electric light plant, and logging equipment. Exactly when the sawmill shut down is not known.

Timberland in the sum of 20,100 acres in Bartlett and Albany still supported some merchantable timber. Two hundred million board feet of spruce saw timber and 250,000 cords of spruce pulpwood were claimed to await harvest by the next owner. It was also noted that the rails of the Bartlett and Albany Railroad were still in place and, although idle and not owned by Bartlett Lumber Company, could be used. Somehow Robert Osgood managed to obtain title to the entire sawmill package for $110,000 on the date of the auction in June 1905. The machinery was then disposed of piecemeal.

After discontinuance of the Bartlett and Albany Railroad, the locomotive was stored at the Maine Central engine house in North Conway for about ten years and then towed away. There is no record of the engine's disposition; it is possible that it was bought back by the builder and rebuilt.

The remainder of the rails of the Bartlett and Albany Railroad were taken up about 1907, and the assumption is that they still belonged to the Boston and Maine Railroad, which had leased them to the railroad's original owner and builder. Over the years, however, it's also been said that some of the rails and track equipment mysteriously vanished at about the same time that the timberland changed ownership.

Constructing the railroad along the steep mountainsides through Crawford Notch required a huge amount of manpower.

SACO VALLEY RAILROAD

Dates: 1892–1898
Owner: Saco Valley Lumber Company
Products hauled: Spruce sawlogs
Length: 6.5 miles

Equipment

Locomotive: *B. C. Garland*—Shay, 25 ton, CN 390
Built by Lima Locomotive Company, 1892
Two truck, cylinders 11" × 12", Wheels 29½"
Bought new 1892
Sold 1898 to Wachsmuth Lumber Company, Bayfield, WI

Cars: Log bunks
Flatcar

CHAPTER FOUR

The Saco Valley Railroad

A GREAT NOTCH IS CUT into the White Mountains, at the origin of the Saco River, at the head of steep mountainsides whose shoulders hug closely to the steep ravine. The heavily wooded side valleys, high rocky slopes, and rushing brooks tumbling over rocky waterfalls sat undiscovered until 1771, when a moose hunter, Timothy Nash, inadvertently stumbled onto the almost impenetrable mountain pass. For years, settlements remained sparse in that imposing wilderness, and lumbering on a major scale would wait for over a century.

Credit is given to the Abel Crawford family for the early development of a rudimentary inn industry in the great notch, and his family name was notched into history when the name of the cut in the mountain range was later changed from White Mountain Notch to Crawford Notch. A rough trail was cut through the notch in the late 1700s, and then a turnpike (toll road) was chartered and cut out in 1803. Freight wagons and horse traders quickly accommodated themselves to this new route between northern New Hampshire and Portland.

The freight and tourist traffic supported a half-dozen inns and taverns in the vicinity of Crawford Notch, two of them in the sparsely settled wilderness confines of the notch. The Willey House, site of the tragic 1826 landslide that took nine lives, was operated as a wayside inn sporadically from 1792 to 1899. The Mount Crawford House was built as a thirty-room tavern at Bemis, at the lower end of the notch, and was constructed soon after the old road was improved to a turnpike in 1803. Lumbering, however, was not part of the scene; the area was too rugged and remote and the Saco River was unsuitable for log drives.

Then came the railroad. The railroad builders sought a route to extend rails from Portland to northern New Hampshire, but many, if not most, engineers

The tall ledge at the top of the Notch required a large rock cut.

reiterated the impossibility of laying a railroad up through the steep and narrow Crawford Notch. In 1864 an attempt was made; a charter was granted to the Portland, White Mountain and Ogdensburg Railroad, but the effort never got off the ground.

Shortly afterwards, in 1867, the Portland and Ogdensburg Railroad was chartered and organized for a grand attempt to push through the notch to northern New England. The Anderson brothers of Maine applied their engineering and promotional skills to achieve the monumental task of laying a railroad bed through that extremely challenging gap in the White Mountain range. In August 1875 the unbelievable was completed, and the line was opened to Fabyan's above the notch. Then came the lumbermen, right on their heels.

No sooner had the newly built P&O Railroad reached the Sawyer River location, between Bartlett and Bemis, than the Daniel Saunders family moved in with their Sawyer River Railroad and the sawmill village of Livermore in 1875. Lumberman Benjamin C. Garland of Jefferson also became active up in the Notch, purchasing 1,100 acres of spruce timber on the east and south slopes of Mt. Willey from James E. Henry in 1884. Four years later he would purchase the standing timber on the Davis Brook and Bemis Brook drainages from the New Hampshire Land Company. The purchase price was $1,400.

A couple of small steam-powered sawmills were set up in the 1880s. Hart and Smith, later reformed as Smith & Company, set up a mill at the end of the Arethusa Falls Road near the Willey House post office, also referred to as Frankenstein Station. Garland is said to have sent logs to this little sawmill by rail. The mill reportedly burned down in 1889. Another small sawmill was set up by Jones and Company about two miles above Notchland (Bemis) at a location soon to become known as Carrigain. This mill was later taken over by Fred H. Garman.

Over on the east side of Crawford Notch there is a small, shallow stream feeding the Saco River which is known as Dry River (formerly Mount Washington River), draining down from Oakes Gulf at the southern base of Mt. Washington's summit cone. *Osgood's White Mountains*, a popular early guidebook dating back to 1876, stated there was little of interest in the narrow confines of the valley except what might attract the fishermen. The Dry River, noted author Moses F. Sweetser, becomes little more than a trickle during drought time, and had formed a broad expanse of gravel near its mouth in the notch valley. Such remote areas occasionally give birth to strange mythical legends, and an old Indian legend had the Dry River valley concealing a great, brilliant, mysterious carbuncle or gem. An occasional party of explorers would hopelessly hunt for it during the early years.

The Portland & Ogdensburg Railroad locomotive Crawford *pauses at the Crawford Notch pass.*

THE PERILS OF WINTER RAILROADING
THROUGH CRAWFORD NOTCH

Winter storms could be severe in Crawford Notch and in the adjoining valleys such as Dry River. Operating a railroad under such wintry conditions could be a large challenge and many harrowing experiences have been related.

In 1894 a blizzard hit Crawford Notch with a temperature approaching 25 degrees below and a fury of blowing and drifting snow that piled up along the Maine Central tracks through the Notch. A freight train attempted to force its way through that night, but became stalled near Mt. Willard, and the two locomotives tried in vain to jam through the high drifts.

The section house was nearby, under the towering cliffs of Mt. Willard, and when the stranded engineer blew the whistle for help, section foreman Jim Mitchell and his crew struggled over to assist. But the wind was blowing a fury and any attempt to shovel through the deep drift was futile. The rear pusher engine was then uncoupled and sent back to Fabyan's to pick up a snowplow.

Upon arrival at Fabyan's, the crew found the plow to be well buried in snow, and it took an hour of shoveling to free it. During the return trip to the stalled train some of the crew had to ride on the plow and three of them huddled on the cow catcher on the nose of the engine. They were encrusted with ice upon arrival.

When reaching the train the engineer of the pusher engine was hampered by limited visibility and crashed into two cars that had been uncoupled. The shackle on the plow also broke, rendering it useless. At that point, the train crew had no choice but to go back with Mitchell to the section house where they were served a good meal while warming their chilled bodies and drying their clothes.

Daylight found the entire train thoroughly snowed under. There were no telephone or telegraph wires connecting the section houses in the notch in those years, thus a messenger was sent on snowshoes back to Fabyan's to inform the Division superintendent of the situation and request help. Another plow and one hundred men with shovels were dispatched to the scene, but it took another 24 hours to free the stranded freight.

(Opposite page, top): *Rail traffic in Crawford Notch was brought to a standstill in this blizzard, identified as occurring in 1884. The location is a half-mile west of the Crawford Notch depot.*

(Opposite page, bottom): *This early view of the small hamlet known as Carrigain shows evidence of a small sawmill. In this view looking northeasterly, the main valley leading to Crawford Notch goes around the cliff to the left, and the view straight ahead is toward the Dry River valley, up which the logging railroad was built.*

An early view of a Portland & Ogdensburg Railroad passenger train in Crawford Notch, halted on the Willey Brook Bridge for the benefit of the photographer.

This narrow Dry River valley was originally granted by the state of New Hampshire in 1810 to the descendents of Thomas Cutts of Saco, Maine, and Richard Conant of Portland, for a mere $340. The six-mile-long wilderness tract of 7,680 acres became known as Cutts Grant. Thomas Cutts, incidentally, had been a leader in the growth of the logging industry along the Saco River in the late eighteenth century and owned many timber tracts along the river.

For another eighty years the tract remained unlogged and undeveloped in any manner as it passed on to ownership by the heirs of Cutts and Conant. Then as Ben Garland and a handful of other lumbermen began to pick away at the slopes of Crawford Notch, the owners felt the opportunity for logging

This logging camp was located in the narrow confines between Dry River and the track of the logging railroad. The track can be seen between the bunkhouse and the deck for loading logs onto the cars.

was ripe. Ben Garland was undoubtedly aware of the rich store of spruce timber in the valley and encouraged the thoughts of selling.

In October 1891 the sale of the standing timber in the Dry River valley was made to the combined interests of Benjamin Garland, Lucius D. Hazen and Charles H. Stevens. Hazen and Stevens were sawmill operators from St. Johnsbury, Vermont, who each owned two or three operating sawmills.

The forty-seven men in this camp crew included the cook and his assistant. Clothing didn't vary much from the traditional gray wool and flannel garments.

The Vermonters supplied the money; Garland offered the local management. Six months later the three of them formed the Saco Valley Lumber Company to own and operate the lumbering activity at Dry River. L. D. Hazen was set up as president, Stevens as director, and Ben Garland as woods superintendent and director.

What the Cutts and Conant heirs had sold these three lumbermen were the standing trees only (stumpage), eight inches and larger on the stump diameter. The lumber company had fifteen years to harvest their purchase and could only cut over the land one time. The estimate on timber volume to be harvested was 100 million board feet. The reported price paid the landowners for the timber was $41,500, or 40 cents per thousand board feet, if the estimate held true.

Logging Railroad

Cutts Grant presented some steep and rugged terrain, but Ben Garland was determined that a railroad was the feasible means to remove the timber as it was harvested. In April 1891 Garland and associates incorporated the Saco Valley Railroad with charter authorization to lay rails from the Fred Garman mill site in Hart's Location on the Maine Central Railroad up Dry River to the far end of Cutts Grant. The railroad charter was obtained six months before the timber was purchased, assuring the investors of a means to pull the logs out of rugged Oakes Gulf at the head of Dry River.

Construction began late in 1892, using rail and track equipment leased from the Boston and Maine Railroad at an annual rental rate of four percent of equipment value. The first 2½ miles of track ran northerly along the gravel plain of the Saco River from the interchange with the Maine Central to the property line of Cutts Grant. This section was over the property of George Morey, who granted a six-rod-wide right-of-way for a rental fee of $62 per year.

The climb up along Dry River was a difficult piece of track to secure in place, crossing the rocky riverbed a dozen times or more over trestlework built upon heavy timber abutments filled with rock. Immense gravel slides and huge boulders were constant impediments. The railroad extended for four miles into Cutts Grant before reaching impenetrable terrain at an elevation of 2,700 feet. The tracks had risen 1,300 feet in elevation since entering the timber property of Cutts Grant, an average grade of about 6½ percent. Total distance on the Saco Valley Railroad was about 6½ miles.

The Saco Valley Railroad was a one-locomotive railroad. A new Shay geared locomotive was delivered to the company in the summer of 1892, a two-truck model that carried the name *B. C. Garland* on the wooden fuel box. The small engine's light weight of 25 tons was probably dictated by caution

over the considerable amount of trestlework. Log cars were the log bunk cars or trucks commonly used in the Saco valley, probably rented from the Boston and Maine Railroad.

An agreement was signed between the Saco Valley Lumber Company, and Otis Smith and Herbert Blanchard of the Bartlett Lumber Company, that the spruce logs would be delivered to the sawmill in Bartlett. Most, if not all, of the logs were apparently delivered to that sawmill about eight miles to the south on the Maine Central. The Saco Valley Lumber Company did not operate a sawmill of its own. Timber cutting began in 1893 with a reported two hundred to three hundred men busy in the logging camps. The annual cut was said to be about eleven to twelve million board feet.

The loaded log cars were brought down to the siding on the Maine Central at Carrigain by the Shay, and left there for a Maine Central locomotive to pick them up for the haul to the Bartlett sawmill. Since these logs were loaded onto log bunk trucks, which had no air brakes, the question remains as to how it was arranged to move these loads over the eight miles of Maine Central track to Bartlett.

It was a steep and worrisome trip down the narrow Dry River valley for the train crew. About 9 A.M. on Thursday, July 16, 1896, engineer George Woodward was descending with a full load behind the Shay. For some reason the brakes failed to hold the weight and the train began to pick up

A log train pauses on one of the many small trestles that carried the track over Dry River.

speed, soon careening out of control. The crew felt there was no choice but to jump.

Engineer George Woodward, a former engineer on the Barre (Vt.) Railroad, leaped and struck his head on a boulder and was killed outright. John T. Murray, the brakeman, age 28, severely injured his head when he hit the ground and died soon afterwards. James Dunn of New Brunswick, Canada, Thomas Walker of Fryeburg, Maine, and Charles Hanson of Hiram, Maine,

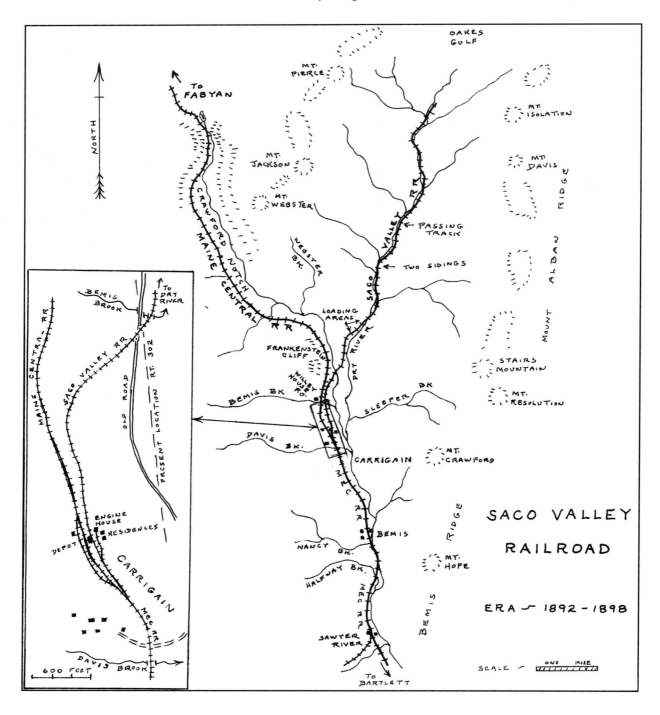

all received injuries when they also "took to the birds." Three other riders remained with the engine and escaped serious injury when the train jumped the rails.

As was occasionally offered on logging railroads, the Saco Valley Railroad would provide excursions for summertime visitors. A flatcar was provided with bench seats and decorated with foliage. Ben Garland would join the group as they were slowly pushed up to one of the logging camps, usually the one at the end of the road. It was customary to treat the visitors to a taste of the camp cook's wares. If they went to the end of the railroad, they were offered the opportunity to walk another three-quarters of a mile to a picturesque waterfall spanning the narrow Dry River ravine.

The Saco Valley Railroad Shay was a lightweight locomotive purchased new in 1892. This photograph was taken at Carrigain in front of the two company residences behind the station.

Carrigain Village

With the establishment of the railroad and logging activity, a settlement quickly grew up around what was once just the location of Fred Garman's sawmill. About five hundred people were once in residence at the boarding house and the several tenement homes on the west side of the Maine Central track, at the end of what later became known as Camp Onion Road. The Saco Valley Lumber Company had their office and company store at this village,

which became known as Carrigain. Charles Harrison was the storekeeper and telegrapher. Added to this were the school, church, Garman mill, miscellaneous company buildings, and a large railroad station with a full-time agent.

The fifteen years granted for timber removal proved to be a bad estimate. By midway through the winter season of 1897–98 operations had ceased. The last trainload of logs came down, probably in February, not quite 5½ years after the first spruce was toppled. Possibly all of the accessible spruce timber had been harvested by that date. If so, the cut fell far short of predictions. Based on the reported harvest of twelve million board feet per year, the Saco Valley Lumber Company would have logged off only about sixty-five million board feet at most.

Another factor leading to the early demise of timber harvesting operations along Dry River may well have been the high maintenance cost of keeping the railroad in operating condition along the narrow valley. Washouts or trestle failures would occur with just about every rise in water flow down the Dry River course. The Appalachian Mountain Club *White Mountain Guide* of 1907 reported that all of the dozen or so trestles had by that date been washed out into oblivion, only nine years since their abandonment. The high cost of operation may well have depleted company resources in the relatively short period of time.

It has been written more than once that logging practices employed along the Dry River were a bold and early step in conservation to sell only the stand-

The large railroad station at Carrigain had a full-time agent, and also housed the store and office of the Saco Valley Lumber Company.

ing timber on a property and to specify only trees eight inches and larger at the stump to be cut. Actually, it was not unusual to sell only the standing trees during that era, although the land under the timber was more often included in sales to timbermen during the 1800s. A minimum stump diameter of eight inches would differ very little from an unrestricted clearcut. After all, an eight-inch diameter at stump level means a tree only six or seven inches in diameter at breast height, and that was hardly a merchantable sawlog size during this era of logging the virgin growth. At best, such a small restriction size might deter the logger from clearing off a few small trees in his way. There is now a

The company store stocked a good supply of woolen blankets and clothing.

thick growth of spruce that has returned to the Dry River valley, as it has on many other tracts once clearcut for old-growth spruce, because nature can readily reclaim what the logger took away.

The once-thriving little settlement of Carrigain also sank into oblivion soon after the Saco Valley Lumber Company ceased operation. Buildings were torn down, the schoolhouse was sold for $12.25 in 1902, and the post office was moved back to Willey House Station. Here, also, nature reclaimed the former forest, and any indication of former civilization is now difficult to locate.

The entire Cutts Grant is now part of the White Mountain National Forest. The heirs of Thomas Cutts sold their ownership rights to the federal government in 1919 and the Richard Conant heirs sold theirs in 1931.

CHAPTER FIVE

The Conway Company
Railroads

THE SWIFT RIVER VALLEY, stretching for over 20 miles westward
from Conway out to Kancamagus Pass, once supported a rich growth
of white pine, spruce and hardwood timber. The two or three small
sawmills along the river had hardly made a dent in the old-growth timber
during the 1800s. The handful of small farms at Passaconaway had only
cleared a little of the land along the Albany Intervale. As the nineteenth century neared its end, many of the large timber tracts in the White Mountains
had been grabbed up by one or another of the timber barons and divested
of the timber growth, but not the land with rich timber stands along the
Swift River.

A seemingly insurmountable hurdle for a lumberman seeking to exploit
the area had been the multitude of ownerships and the difficult land titles to
deal with. An accessible, solidified timber tract under a single ownership did
not exist in a large enough acreage. When Daniel Saunders of Lawrence,
Massachusetts, came into possession of the 80,000-acre Elkins Grant north
of Swift River in the 1860s, he was seeking an access route along the Swift
River valley. A charter was obtained from the state in 1874 to build a railroad
up the Swift River to be known as the Swift River Railroad. Failure to commence construction within ten years resulted in a revived charter in 1887, but
still no effort was made to build the railroad. The reason seems to have been
the difficulty in obtaining land titles. And while Saunders did eventually find
another route into his tract, the Swift River valley remained practically
untouched.

By the end of the nineteenth century, three logging railroads had been built
in the region north of Swift River; two had finished their mission and were

This small steam-powered sawmill operated in the Swift River area in the late 1800s. Posing for the photo are members of the mill crew.

gone. However, events and certain people were now coming together that would change the face of the Swift River country and bring in the largest logging railroad ever to be built along the Saco.

George B. James and his land-holding New Hampshire Land Company had been buying up large timber tracts, some of which extended over into the Swift River drainage. At the same time, A. Crosby Kennett of Conway had been accumulating ownerships in the same region, as well as in other towns, during the late 1800s. Kennett had made his mark on the Conway industrial scene, purchasing a box shop and a spool mill as well as some industrial property along the Boston and Maine Railroad.

Then from the upper echelon of Wall Street capitalists in New York City there appeared Oakleigh Thorne, the man with the finances that could put things all together. Consequently, there began a period of financial and legal shenanigans that would fill a volume in an attempt to chronicle; these deals and maneuverings of Thorne and Kennett kept the big-city lawyers busy for years.

The timber properties of Kennett and James were gathered together in 1901 under the cloak of a company known as the White Mountain Paper Company. At the same time, this new company had made some large investments in a proposed process of manufacturing paper with the use of salt water, but the venture did not succeed, forcing the large project into bankruptcy in 1903.

Thorne and associates were able to ride through a rough period of reor-

The Russell Colbath House was once part of the small remote settlement known as Passaconaway. The historic building is now a U.S. Forest Service information center.

ganization and to subsequently place the large accumulation of timber holdings and industrial property into a holding company known as the Publisher's Paper Company. This company was actually an enterprise set up by the timber barons to facilitate legal assaults on the old-growth timber of the White Mountains. From this jumble of legal maneuverings emerged the Conway Company, later known as the Conway Lumber Company, a capable and prosperous lumber-manufacturing firm that was to remain on the scene for thirteen years before its timber supply became exhausted.

Oakleigh Thorne set himself up as president of Conway Company and, from all appearances, treated his lumber company, and the three logging railroads that were to be built, as his playthings for recreation. This financial tycoon would occasionally arrive at Conway from his 27 Wall Street office in a most unusual manner, perched on a custom-built running board seat on the right side of his chauffeur-driven Packard roadster.

The Conway Company sawmill was a steel-framed, three-story structure.

THE CONWAY COMPANY'S LARGE SAWMILL

Built in 1907, the Conway Company had one of the largest sawmills in the northeastern United States. The mill location was on the edge of Pequawket Pond on the southwestern edge of Conway village, on what is now known as Hobbs Street.

The sawmill was a 20,000-square-foot, three-story, heavy steel-framed structure with an equally as large sorting and shipping shed attached to the outfeed end on the west side. The principal machinery was on the second floor, with the saw filing room on the third level and above the head saws. The ceiling area of the first floor was a maze of shafting, pulleys and belts, with the machines above powered by belts protruding through the floor. This arrangement eliminated exposed overhead belts in the working area as found in most mills of this era.

As the long tree-length logs entered the mill from the conveyor they were cut into log lengths from 20 to 40 feet long by means of a circular saw that rose up from below the floor level.

There were two "head rigs" or log carriages that would wholly or partially break down the

The log carriage on the left side of the mill was a Lane No. 2½ made in Montpelier, Vermont. It was a fast-acting steam-powered saw rig that would handle spruce logs up to 40 feet in length. The two riders on the carriage are George Culbroth and Tom Ledger; the dogger on the left has his left hand on a cross-acting dog, which grips the log, and the setter on the right has his right hand on the double-action back set, which moves the log out for the specified thickness of the saw cut. Sawyer Frank Culbroth sits at his controls next to the band saw and would signal with his fingers how many inches to set out the log. Also identifiable is Bill Culbroth, standing behind the carriage.

The filing room for repairing and sharpening the band and circular saws was on the third floor over the sawing machinery, allowing the band saw to be pulled up to the room without excess handling. The filer in the photo is Arthur Goskin; Arthur Sawyer did the saw repairs.

logs into lumber by means of large band saws. The larger carriage, the "long side," was capable of holding large logs up to 40 feet in length, while the shorter carriage, the "short side," handled the logs under 20 feet. Though on opposite sides of the entrance, both carriages fed lumber into the same set of edgers and other machinery. The steam-driven log carriage had three men who rode it during the rapid, jerky passes through the saw. One man would set the log ahead before each consecutive cut, moving ahead the distance he was signaled to do so by the sawyer, who controlled the carriage motion and the steam-driven log turner. The other two men were "doggers," who quickly set the dogs to hold the log firmly. The short carriage on the other side of the mill had only two riders.

From the headsaw, the lumber moved on powered rolls through the circular resaws, edgers and trimmers. In the left foreground is a cant to be fed through the resaw, which is a bank of circular saws. One of the operators is identified as Jeff Boutlier. Planers at the back end surfaced one edge of the dimension stock.

Powered rolls moved the lumber and waste cuttings through the long mill ahead. A circular resaw to break down cants coming from the head saw, as well as the edgers and trimmers, were arranged in a parallel series of machinery lines the length of the large building.

The sawmill machinery and practices of this era were not efficient as far as lumber recovery was concerned, especially with a huge operation such as the Conway mill. The heavy edgings and thick slabs would leave the mill about halfway down, conveyed sideways on conveyor chains about 6 inches above the floor and passing through overhead slasher saws which cut the mill waste into four-foot lengths.

Passing before men sorting the waste cuttings, the straight, clear edgings were placed on other conveyors to take them to stripping saws that made lath. Other appropriate-sized edgings and slabs were sent on another conveyor to the kin-dling bundling mill. The remainder of the waste wood was fed through a massive, cast-iron hog with heavy short knives to reduce the wood to chips that were then conveyed outside to be fed into the boiler.

The steam engine was located in a separate brick house for the boiler and engine room. Seth Berry is the engineer.

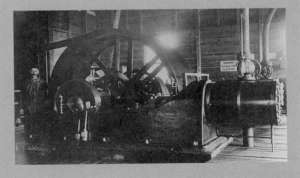

Sawmill superintendent L. D. Goulding was on hand to oversee daily operation of the mill. Seldom seen, however, were Vice President L. S. Tainter, Treasurer F. W. Black, or Sales Manager J. C. Kennedy.

Plans for the logging railroad began even before the dust had settled from the years of corporate legal manipulations. In 1903, Kennett, James and other associates obtained a charter for a railroad to run from the location of Kennett's spool mill in Conway westward to a location in Waterville or Livermore. It was to be known as the Swift River Railroad.

Construction of the large sawmill began in 1907 and operations began in the later part of that year. The mill became one of the largest to be found in the northeastern United States, sawing 100–125 thousand board feet per day, or 30 million board feet a year. There were days when the mill put out as much as 140,000 board feet.

A sawmill of this production level required a large supply of logs on hand to assure continued production. The hot pond was formed from an enclosed area within Pequawket Pond. It was heated by steam exhaust and used year-round to wash and sort the logs. After the winter logging season, there might be forty million board feet or more of logs in the pond area, piled from bank to bank, including tree-length logs seventy-five feet or longer. When spring arrived and the railroad had to cease operations temporarily, the large yard crew was no longer needed. In April 1914, for example, many of the log pond workers left to join up on the Connecticut River log drive.

Sawmills of this era were quite labor intensive and, with a local labor force unable to fulfill the needs, the company brought in many Polish and Russian immigrants to work the prerequisite ten-hour work days. Few of these men spoke English and injuries were common, but—as was common in the indus-

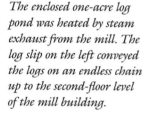

The enclosed one-acre log pond was heated by steam exhaust from the mill. The log slip on the left conveyed the logs on an endless chain up to the second-floor level of the mill building.

Workers in the mill pond move logs over to the log slip.

try at this time—the welfare and even the lives of the workers were given insufficient consideration and safety measures were unknown. The large hog used to grind up the waste wood into fuel would sometimes jam at the in-feed with too much wood entering the throat. The Polish worker feeding the machine was told to jump on the jam in order to force it down into the hog; that is, until the day that he fell down through and had his arm chewed to shreds by the knives in the hog.

There was also a great influx of French Canadian workers for the mill and the woods. Conway had, until this time, been a small New England village with a strictly Yankee populace. This invasion of new nationalities became somewhat overwhelming for the older residents. Local historians claim truthfulness to the story about the group of locals discussing whether or not they liked French Canadians and the statement by a woman who said she couldn't tell yet because the only one she knew was Pat Murphy.

Patrick Murphy was an overly fat Irishman who operated the cut-off saw, which cut the tree-length logs to proper lengths as they entered the mill. One winter day, Murphy walked onto the platform at the top of the log slip, leaned against the flimsy railing, and toppled down into a snow pile thirty feet below. A steam pipe helped to break his fall and prevented serious injury. Ike Tewksbury, another mill employee, had an even more humiliating accident. While tending the fires at the mill power plant he let go with a powerful sneeze, sending a complete set of false teeth into the fire.

The sawyers who operated the large band saw (head saw) were included in the elite among the rank of employees. Frank Culbroth was the sawyer on the long log side and Will Culbroth the sawyer on the short log side. The two of them claimed to have sawn the first and last logs to enter the mill.

The lumber platform at the outfeed end of the sawmill is full for the loading of flatcars. In the center rear is the power plant and waste burner, and on the right is the tall kindling mill.

THE KINDLING MILL

———◆◆◆———

As the 1907 construction of the new sawmill was proceeding, the Conway Company worked out an agreement in June with the White Mountain Kindling Company to set up a kindling mill on a site adjacent to the sawmill. Suitable kindling wood was removed from the sawmill waste conveyor and placed on a conveyor to the kindling bundling operation.

The bundling was done by a large work force of young women. The kindling pieces were cut back to three feet in length and held by a steam clamp as the bundle was tied with tarred hemp cord. The kindling mill had forty employees and operated twenty-four steam clamps.

The kindling wood company paid Conway Company 75 cents a cord and sold the bundles in the Boston market for three dollars a cord for domestic kindling to start coke fires. The foreman of the kindling mill was Warren Munsey.

The sawmill log yard proved to be a dangerous work place also. Frank Towle ran the steam donkey engine and sling, which unloaded the railroad cars and placed the load on one of the piles in the pond. On one occasion he interpreted the helper's hand signals incorrectly and dragged the bundle of logs over a worker, killing him. Also, in March 1908, Benjamin Fennimore was killed when caught between two swinging logs while unloading some log cars. The following year Joseph Withers broke a leg while unloading a car. George Thibodeau, a brakeman on the log train, fell between the log cars while switching in the yard; the car wheel decapitated him. On another occasion, one of the brakemen set the car brakes too tightly while switching and the reach (or connecting timber) between the cars broke off and fell down. The end caught up against a tie, and it jackknifed the car over and off the rails, causing the other cars to topple over like dominoes.

The first logs started to arrive over the new company railroad early in 1907. In March a published report indicated there was already five million board feet of logs in the mill pond and another two million waiting along the new Swift River Railroad. Sawmill production got into full rhythm by late summer, but there were a host of discouraging and costly problems encountered during the start-up, and as a result, Oakleigh Thorne importuned A. Crosby Kennett to help out with management for a while. Kennett agreed to do so for one year.

Kennett, as mentioned earlier, was one of the local property owners who allied with Thorne and George James to create the huge land ownership that made Conway Company possible. Kennett also sold the new corporation the industrial land where the new sawmill was built, as well as his nearby

Logs were unloaded in the yard so that they could be pulled into the log pond off to the left. The yard boss was William Withers, later replaced by Neal Bohan. Examination of the butt ends of the spruce logs reveals that the trees were felled by axe alone, no saw.

box factory and his spool mill, which he had operated successfully for many years.

A. C. Kennett remained at the management helm until October of 1908, when he severed all connections with Conway Company. Opinions and recollections have been divided among the old-timers and historians of Conway as to whether Kennett's efforts were particularly creditable in launching the company on to success, and as to whether or not his role as land agent was improper and grossly self-serving. At any rate, after the first year of trials and tribulations, the mill did well for its owners.

Although the mill sawed primarily spruce and white pine, hardwood was also sawn in later years. In July 1912 a hardwood lumber department was added to the Boston sales office. By then Kennett had developed a sorting system for the clearcuttings of hardwood. A cone-shaped conveyor carried the cuttings in front of working girls, who would sort the pieces as they passed

CONWAY COMPANY RAILROADS

Swift River Railroad

Dates: 1906–1916
Products hauled: Softwood and hardwood sawlogs, occasional passengers
Length: 26 miles

EQUIPMENT — LOCOMOTIVE ROSTER

No.	Type	Bldr.	Bldr. No.	Date Built	Wgt.	Cyl. & Drivers	Source	Disposition
1 (1st)	4-4-0	Brooks	944	1883		17" × 24"	B&M #932	Destroyed in engine house fire
	(used in construction of railroad)							
1 (2nd)	2-4-2ST	Baldwin	30449	1907		15" × 24"–48"	New 1907	1915 to Berlin Mills
2	0-4-4 Forney Class S-8	Rhode Island	25885	1891	27	14" × 20"–49"	NY NH&H #2135, bought 1906	Unknown
3	2-4-2ST	Baldwin	13693	1893	35	14" × 24"–46"	EB&L #2, bought 1907	Mill in Lawrence, Mass.
4	2-4-2ST	Baldwin	7794	1886	25	14" × 24"–44"	Success Pond RR, bought 1912	1920 to Sawyer River RR
	(the former *J. E. Henry* on Zealand Valley RR)							

ROLLING STOCK

Log cars — log bunks and flatcars; Wedge plow; Flanger; Two 4-wheel cabooses by. There was another small mill where the white birch was sawn into blanks for the spool and peg mills in the area.

During the World War I years the mill worked day and night to fill the essential war needs, though usually just one head saw operated during the night shift. Many days resulted in as many as one hundred railroad cars being fully loaded with lumber ready for shipment out on the Boston & Maine Railroad. The first eight days of May 1914, in fact, resulted in a record shipment of timber product—760,000 board feet of lumber and 490,000 laths.

The Conway Company Railroads

From the very inception of the enterprise, the plans of Oakleigh Thorne and associates were to move their logs to the mill by railroad transport. Large land

---

Rocky Branch Railroad

Dates: 1908–1914
Products hauled: Spruce sawlogs
Length: 11½ miles

EQUIPMENT—LOCOMOTIVE ROSTER

No.	Type	Bldr.	Bldr. No.	Date Built	Wgt.	Source	Disposition
5	2-truck tapered boiler	Climax	2128	1907–08	57	New 1908	1910 to Brown Co., Millsfield RR
	Purchased back again from Brown Co. in 1915 in exchange for Conway Co. #1 (2nd) Baldwin. Remembered then as #1 (3rd). Sold 1919 to Brown Co. for use in Trois Pistoles, Quebec.						
5 (2nd)	2-truck flat top boiler	Climax	2129	9/1910	50	New 1910	1921 to Great Northern Paper Co. for SL & St. J. RR
	Wrecked 1913, rebuilt at Portland Co.						

CARS
See Swift River Railroad

East Branch Railroad

Dates: 1916–1920
Product hauled: Spruce sawlogs
Length: 13 miles

EQUIPMENT
Locomotives and cars: Same as Rocky Branch Railroad

Engine No. 2, the Rhode Island–built Forney, waits near the engine house in 1908.

ownerships of unknown acreages had been put together along the Swift River and north of Conway along the Rocky Branch and East Branch of the Saco River in the towns of Jackson and Bartlett. Three different railroad operations were to be required over the thirteen-year period of the company's lifespan.

The company's locomotive roster was an impressive one. Seven, possibly eight, locomotives were acquired over the years, while on at least one other occasion locomotives were leased from the Boston and Maine or the Maine Central Railroads for seasonal use. Track laying began in the mill yard and up the Swift River valley in 1906, and the first two locomotives arrived that year. An old Brooks 4-4-0 was picked up for use in construction of the Swift River

The second No. 1, a Baldwin saddletank. The 2-4-2 wheel arrangement was quite popular among New England railroad loggers.

line, and a secondhand 0-4-4 Rhode Island–built Forney was acquired to begin the hauls along Swift River. The Brooks, however, was lost soon afterwards in an engine house fire at Conway.

Two more locomotives were added in 1907: a new Baldwin saddletank and a well-used Baldwin from the East Branch and Lincoln Railroad over on the other side of the mountain. Two new Climax geared locomotives were purchased (in 1908 and 1910) and finally, in 1912, a little Baldwin saddletank, once the prized possession of timber baron James E. Henry, was added. Thus there were known to have been five rod locomotives and two geared Climaxes. In addition, there may also have been another Baldwin and another Climax, although no records exist to confirm this.

The log cars used by Conway Company were the individual log trucks with a "reach," or connecting timber, coupled between each pair. The company had at least forty-five sets of these log trucks, which had become quite popular among the loggers in the White Mountains. The Boston and Maine is reported to have owned over eleven hundred log bunks at one point in the early 1900s, inheriting them from the smaller railroads that they had gobbled up. These were made available to the logging operators on a lease arrangement.

Other former Boston and Maine equipment used by the company included a wedge plow, a flanger, two 4-wheel cabooses, tool cars, and flat cars. Conway Company loaded the logs by hand at the woods end and unloaded with a cable sling in the mill yard.

The well-traveled little 25-ton Baldwin, formerly the J. E. Henry, *was purchased by Conway Company in 1912 and numbered "4." Conductor Phil Robarge is seated on the front end, and in the cab is Eddie Parent in the window and engineer Rob Bennet standing in the doorway.*

Seated on the nose of the second No. 1 Baldwin in the Conway mill yard is maintenance engineer Seth Berry (in center), who is flanked by conductor Thomas Hamilton and Herbert Moore. The photo dates back to 1900.

The company built an engine house in Conway near the point where the Swift River Railroad crossed over the Boston and Maine tracks. A fire in the engine house during the early years destroyed the old Brooks locomotive, and a three-stall engine house was rebuilt. Then on March 5, 1914, excitement in the village alarmed many early risers as a 6:30 A.M. fire destroyed the engine house again. Fortunately, all of the locomotives were out shifting or coaling up.

The three Conway Company railroads are here treated separately and, as will be noted, were each operated differently.

Swift River Railroad (1906–1916)

The Swift River Railroad had been chartered and incorporated back in 1903, preparatory to an assault on this huge area of old-growth timber in the Swift River valley. In April 1906 the Boston and Maine Railroad signed an agreement with the Swift River Railroad (and with parent corporation Publishers Paper Company) to furnish the track material, the rails, fish plates and switches. The annual rental fee was three percent of the value, and the secondhand rail and other material were valued at $20 per ton. At the end of operations, the Swift River Railroad was to remove the rail at their own cost and return it to the B&M.

At the mill yard end, the Swift River track had to cross over the Boston and Maine line in order to extend up the river valley. In April 1907 the company reached an agreement with the B&M to construct the Swift River track across the B&M at grade, with the Boston and Maine to do the construction at a cost to the Conway Company of $2,750. The company also agreed to pay the cost of the track and the ball signal, keep the signal in repair, pay for the services of a signal tender, and be responsible for the removal of ice and snow at the crossing.

The masthead ball, or ball target signal, authorized the Swift River Railroad train to cross over when displaying one ball by day or one red light by night. At the same time, any Boston and Maine train would be held back at the crossing.

The railroad roadbed was well built, with a gentle grade the whole length of the valley following the course of the Swift River. Even the spur lines followed an easy grade. For that reason, it's obvious why there is no report or existing photographs of a geared locomotive being used on the Swift River

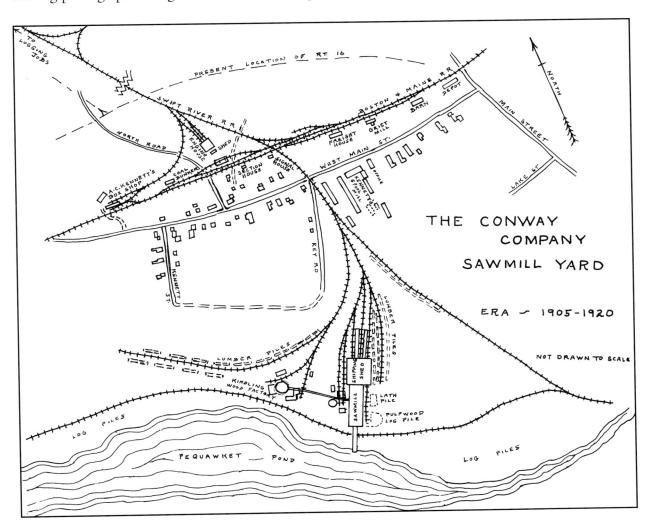

THE CONWAY COMPANY SAWMILL YARD

ERA ~ 1905-1920

NOT DRAWN TO SCALE

The ball target signal was
used to regulate the trains
where the Swift River
Railroad crossed over the
Boston & Maine. B&M
engine No. 116 is seen just
headed south from the
Conway station.

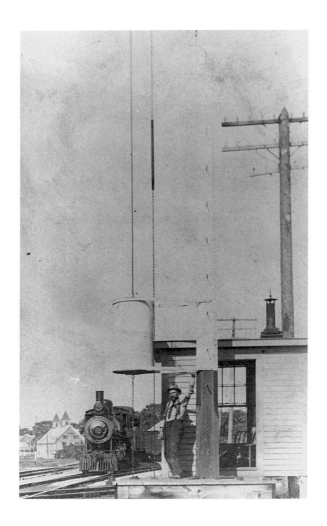

During the building of the
Swift River Railroad, the
Conway Company set up
a construction camp at
Passaconaway for the Polish
laborers.

line; three rod locomotives did most of the work. Engine No. 2, the 0-4-4, was used primarily as a yard switcher.

The railroad construction crew had a large contingent of immigrant Polish workers setting up work camps along the Swift River. Joe Duffy was one of the construction bosses, also Charles Parent, on both the Swift River and East Branch lines. Parent's son, Eddie, spent many years working on logging railroads in the White Mountains, starting as a brakeman at age 16 and then as engineer for Conway Company, followed by many years as engineer on the Beebe River Railroad and the East Branch and Lincoln Railroad. Other engineers for the Conway Company included Fred Lane on the woods locomotive and Ed Knight on the yard shifter. Included among the conductors were Frank Christian, Tom Hamilton and Phil Robarge.

Reports vary on the length of trackage on the Swift River line, but measurements on the map indicate an estimated distance of about nineteen miles from the Conway mill to the west end of the trunk line below Mt. Kancamagus. The side tracks and spurs added almost seven additional miles of track, making a grand total of about twenty-six miles. The longest spur line was up along Douglas Brook to the Bear Mountain operation, with the rails laid up the brook bed on pilings.

Construction on the initial portion of the Swift River Railroad was completed early in 1907. The first trainload of logs to the new sawmill arrived that summer.

There were at least three track wyes, one at each end and one at Passaconaway, which meant that the engineer rarely had to push his train of log cars.

Locomotive No. 2 pauses with a loaded train on some low trestlework along Swift River near Blueberry Hill.

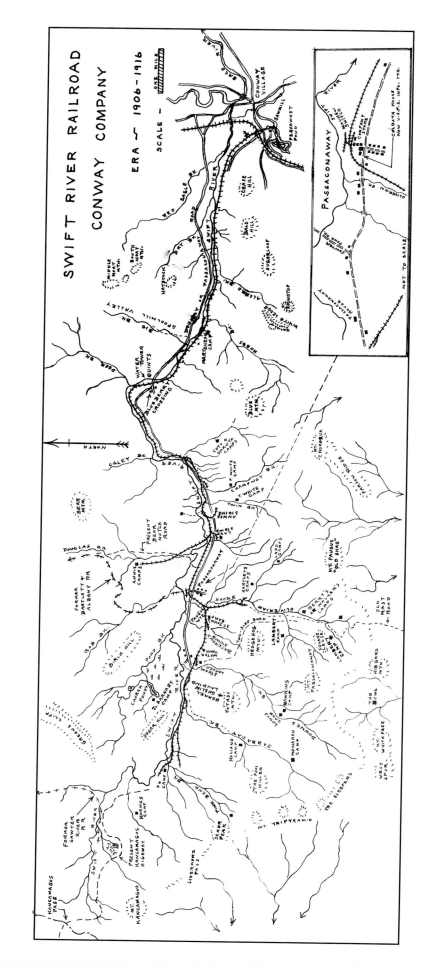

The track of the Swift River Railroad hugged close to the riverbed, as in this location near Rocky Gorge.

The company's first Baldwin saddletank came to the railroad new in 1907. The log car contains a mixture of log species, some of which are not sawlogs. Standing on the left is Ozzie Wheeler.

A trainload consisted of 20–25 carloads, each with about 8,000 board feet of logs, averaging possibly 175,000 board feet per trainload. During the hauling seasons there would often be three trainloads per day hauled into the mill. Riders would be carried if they had a pass, with Blueberry Crossing being a destination for many.

Accidents on a logging railroad were often peculiar to that type of railroading. The Conway Company rigged up a flanger under an old boxcar; the flanger was a blade used to dig snow and ice out from between the rails. The flanger was raised or lowered by means of a pole (which was set upon a fulcrum inside the boxcar) and raised whenever approaching an obstruction between the rails. On one occasion the operator in the boxcar was sitting on the pole and failed to observe a switch coming up. When the flanger blade hit the switch the operator was thrown up against the car ceiling, killing him. Another time, a conductor named Lynn was injured when he was thrown from the car.

Logging in the Swift River Valley

The parent corporation, the Publishers Paper Company, owned the timberland and, although it was strictly a land holding company for the same owners that controlled the Conway Company, the logs sent to Conway had to be measured and accounted for on the records. William Morrison was the head scaler for Publishers Paper Company.

The initial timber harvesting on the Swift River was in the vicinity of the

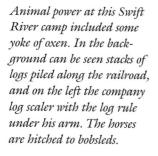

Animal power at this Swift River camp included some yoke of oxen. In the background can be seen stacks of logs piled along the railroad, and on the left the company log scaler with the log rule under his arm. The horses are hitched to bobsleds.

PERILS OF A BRAKEMAN
ON THE SWIFT RIVER RAILROAD

Brakemen on a logging railroad had a particularly dangerous occupation as they made their footing along a twisting, grinding, wet or icy load of moving logs in daylight or darkness.

The New Hampshire Railroad Commission, in an official report concerning an accident involving a log train brakeman in 1900, once stated: "for it is to be said that the business in which he is engaged is an extra hazardous one, that the machinery and methods in use in moving logs appear to be primitive and crude, and to afford little chance of even the most prudent brakeman to do the work in safety . . . we must expect similar casualties in which the best of men lose their lives."

That was the case with Homer Bates, who had his leg crushed while working on a Swift River Railroad log train.

The Conway Compny used link-and-pin couplers on all operations, another danger for the brakeman, as he often had to hold the pin with his hand while the locomotive spaced the distance between cars. Sometimes the engineer had to bump the cars to knock down the pin being held by the brakeman. Brakeman Frank Page had two fingers and part of his hand crushed while coupling on the Swift River in that manner.

Spruce Hill Camp, located near the stop on the logging railroad known as Quints. Jack Pickett was the camp boss at Spruce Hill.

Timber harvesting for the Conway Company was done for the most part by logging contractors rather than by loggers on the company payroll. One of the largest contractors to work for Conway Company was the Fernald–Woodward Company of Berlin, New Hampshire. Other contractors included Wilbur Marshall (also known as Marshall Lumber Company) and Andrew J. Richardson, who failed financially while operating the camp on Champney Brook.

The Conway Company woods superintendent would select the location of the loading sites for the railroad cars and keep a close eye on the activities of the contractor. Serving as woods bosses over the years were William (Win) Schoppe, Ike Thurston and Tom Blaney.

From 1907 through 1909 there were as many as a thousand men in the woods working out of ten to twelve camps scattered throughout the Swift River valley. Many of the trees would be cut during the summer months, skidded out, and piled up along the sled roads, with as much as 150,000 board feet at one skidway. It would be winter before the sleds could haul out the large loads over the well-manicured and iced sled roads. Most of the railroading

A teamster and his team of horses negotiates a fairly steep grade with a large load on the bobsled. With a bobsled, the rear ends of the logs are dragged on the ground to create a braking action on the slope. Note the upright bunting driven in along the curves to keep the load within the road. This slope has been clearcut.

was done in the winter, although some timber was hauled by rail during the summer and fall months when the timber was close enough to yard or skid to the rail siding without the use of a two-sled.

It was the policy during this era to clearcut all of the trees when logging the steep slopes. The loggers long ago noticed that any spruce left standing on the thin soils of the exposed slopes would likely be windthrown after all of the larger trees had been removed. Thus they cut all the softwood. All of the hardwood trees and other unmerchantable material would also be felled on the slopes, allowing the loggers to roll the long spruce logs over the bed of fallen trees down to the sled road below. The area would become a veritable firetrap for years to come. The practice described above was usually confined to the slopes where the logs could be rolled downhill.

The contracting company, Fernald–Woodward, only stayed with Conway Company for about three years, primarily because of a major contract dispute. The contract signed by O. W. Fernald on October 27, 1907, covered a volume of twenty-seven million board feet of timber to be logged and loaded onto the Swift River Railroad. But it also included the commonly stated provision that a portion of each year's cut had to be made in the least accessible parts of the assigned harvest area. This was not an unusual contract demand; loggers had been known to cut off the areas easiest to reach and then skip out before finishing the contract. It was a contract provision, however, that was to result in extensive legal problems for both parties and a permanent break between them.

Apparently the Fernald–Woodward Company was experiencing some overwhelming difficulties with the provision. Long, expensive sled roads had been built into the remote areas, but after three years of logging activity the Conway Company claimed that Fernald–Woodward was not cutting enough remote timber and was thus in violation of the contract.

Conway Company filed suit for cancellation of the contract and Fernald–Woodward Company brought a countersuit for payment of money withheld by Conway Company for logs that had already been delivered. By order of the court, estimates had to be made by a neutral party regarding the amount of roads built and the cost involved. Then a cruise, or careful estimate, had to be made of the timber still standing in the contract area, a three-week project. The litigation lasted almost ten years, but the resulting verdict awarded Fernald–Woodward over $40,000 for contract work performed.

During World War I, labor became scarce, especially for the tough work demanded in the woods. In hopes of alleviating the shortage, contractor Wilbur Marshall, Sherman Adams of the Parker–Young Company, and Perley Churchill traveled out to Des Moines, Iowa, to bring back some reject soldiers for use in the woods. The project didn't work out, however. Since the men were technically still in the Army, the lumber companies did not have complete control over them and they reportedly contributed more trouble than assistance.

This camp of the Fernald–Woodward Company was located along Sabbaday Brook during the winter of 1907–08. There are over fifty men visible in the photo.

THE RESOURCEFUL ANTICS
OF A CAMP BOSS

The following story was related by Charles Edward Beals Jr. in his book *Passaconaway in the White Mountains*, published in 1916. Old-time logging stories have a way of becoming amplified over the years, but Beals presented this account as a true occurrence. It occurred in a logging camp up on the Swift River during his time in the area.

It seems that the crew in one of the logging camps refused to work one Sunday. There had previously been a couple of stormy days followed by a holiday, and the camp boss needed them to work after three days of loafing. He berated the men, stating that it had been costly to feed them. A few gave in, but most refused to leave the bunkroom.

The camp boss, not one to accept defeat, informed them that they would have five minutes to clear out and head for the woods. None stirred after four minutes, but the resolute camp boss was still not to be outdone. He placed a stick of dynamite under the camp floor where the men were sitting, lit it, and informed the crew. The camp quickly emptied, and the boss calmly walked over and stamped out the fuse.

Spruce was the primary species harvested, cut tree-length for loading onto the railroad cars. Lengths were forty feet and greater. Hemlock was harvested also on all three of the company railroad operations. The Swift River operation, however, had a resource not found in the other areas of company logging—exceptionally large white pine. This was the area picked over by the mast log cutters many years before, and there were still many large pine still standing when the Conway Company moved in, especially in the Pine Bend Brook area.

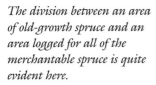

The division between an area of old-growth spruce and an area logged for all of the merchantable spruce is quite evident here.

The Kennett box shop was located along the Boston & Maine track and had its own sidings.

Logging contractor Wilbur Marshall had a crew along Pine Bend Brook during the 1915–16 season. They supposedly cut a large pine that required sixteen pair of horses to haul out. It was said that the entire camp crew stood on the butt log for a photograph.

Harry Marsh of Colebrook, New Hampshire, was scaling for Wilbur Marshall at that time, and Marsh once recalled a large pine cut at Pine Bend by lumberjack Bill Curtin, possibly the same tree mentioned above. The butt log was six feet in diameter and thirty-four feet long. The entire tree made a trainload, but the first three logs had to be notched to fit inside the stakes on the log car. Photographs were taken, according to Marsh, but have apparently since been lost.

Hardwood logs were cut to some extent. A. C. Kennett had established a box factory alongside the B&M track in 1897 and, when the Swift River Railroad was constructed, a siding was built for rail delivery of logs to the box shop. The factory made box shooks, using about 3.5 million board feet of hardwood logs annually.

A. C. Kennett also had a spool mill near the Conway Company sawmill that consumed about four thousand cords of white birch annually, ranking it among the largest thread and silk spool factories in the world. The white birch bolts were hauled out on railroad flatcars.

Passaconaway

The establishment of the Swift River Railroad transformed the quiet little farming settlement of Passaconaway into a bustling headquarters for the logging activity. The small inn once known as the Carrigain House was purchased by Conway Company, used for housing company officials, and a store was added on. Freight sheds were also put up, as were a number of small residences. The settlement supported over fifteen hundred active inhabitants, at least two schoolhouses, a post office, and several boarding homes. There

The company store at Passaconaway was renovated from an older building. Neal Crouse and Charles Beals are seen working on the roof.

might be several trains a day to Passaconaway, and any riders had to have a pass.

Many French Canadian woodsmen and Italian laborers, some with families, were drawn to the area when the logging began. A settlement of shacks was built for the loggers at the lower or east end of the intervale, near Champney Falls, and a number of other log shacks with tar-papered roofs were put up along the banks of various brooks. The settlement of shacks at the east end of the intervale was known as The Cottages.

A short distance down the Swift River from The Cottages was the old William Allen sawmill, which the Conway Company purchased and closed

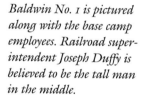

Baldwin No. 1 is pictured along with the base camp employees. Railroad superintendent Joseph Duffy is believed to be the tall man in the middle.

down. The mill dam on Swift River was converted into a bridge for log sleds that were hauling timber down off Bear Mountain.

The railroad spur that went south from the Paugus wye for about a mile to Hartley's Camp was an unusually busy track. They called the loading area at the end of the spur the Great Landing. Logs were landed here from the large area drained by Oliverian Brook, covered by seven logging camps.

Logging costs were high in the Oliverian Brook valley, sometimes reaching a cost of $21 per thousand board feet stacked at the landing. With spruce lumber then worth $10.50 per thousand board feet, dressed four sides, it's obvious that some of the contractors took quite a loss.

The logging contractors were not the only parties that sometimes suffered strained relationships with the Conway Company. From 1907 to mid-1909 the company had the Fernald–Woodward Company cut timber within the area of disputed ownership that Charles G. Saunders laid claim upon, as related in the chapter on the Sawyer River Railroad. The Conway Company loggers had cut seven million board feet before Saunders eventually took action and instituted a lawsuit in December 1908, demanding trespass damages of $250,000 from Conway Company.

The sheriff was ordered to attach logs and cordwood to a value of

The little Rhode Island–built No. 2 was one of the work-horses on the Swift River line.

$260,000, and on December 10 over eight million board feet of logs stacked railside were attached in the Swift River valley. The following day another three million board feet stacked at the Conway Company mill yard received the sheriff's notice. What then transpired is unknown, but the case was finally put to rest in 1913 with the court's decision upholding ownership by Saunders.

With so many men in the woods it is not surprising that there was an occasional forest fire in the valley. In October 1908 a fire near Passaconaway brought a few men up on the train from the mill to extinguish the blaze. Another fire in 1912 was much more destructive, having been started in the notch between Mts. Paugus, Hedgehog and Passaconaway by university students on a camping trip. Conway Company sent crews up on the train and all of the logging camps sent over their lumberjacks to assist company fire warden Fred Howe. In all, some two hundred men worked to contain the blaze. Also, in June 1915, hundreds of acres of forest were left in ashes from another fire over on the east side of Paugus.

Ten years of intense logging had drained the Swift River valley of most of the merchantable softwood timber when the company closed down the Swift River Railroad in 1916. For the last two years of operation the Publishers Paper Company had been seriously considering sale of the land to the U.S. Forest Service, and the loggers were encouraged to leave nothing standing of any value.

Conway Company had already been railroad logging up on the Rocky Branch of the Saco River for eight years prior to closing the Swift River line, and was starting to build a railroad up the East Branch, when activity ceased on the Swift River. In the summer of 1916 the rails were pulled up along the Swift River.

There is little remaining in the valley now to testify to this busy era. All that's left of the once bustling Passaconaway settlement is one house—the Russell Colbath House at the U.S. Forest Service historic site—a small cemetery adjacent to the house, and a few camps built since that active time. Much of the Swift River Railroad roadbed was buried under construction of the Kancamagus Highway.

The Rocky Branch Railroad (1908–1914)

A sawmill the size of the Conway Company mill, cutting thirty million board feet annually, demanded a consistent input of logs. Even a logging operation the size of that along the Swift River would probably be incapable of satisfying the need when considering the seasonal nature of logging and railroad operations in the woods. But the Conway Company had the solution; large areas of virgin timber had been acquired by the Publishers Paper Company in the mountainous region of the town of Jackson and adjacent towns. So, in 1907, the same year that the Swift River Railroad was completed, work began on a railroad up into the remote valley drained by the Rocky Branch River.

The Rocky Branch Railroad received an incorporation charter early in 1906, and in July 1907 the surveyors moved up into the long, narrow valley to lay out a course for a roadbed. In that same month the Conway Company recorded a complex agreement with both the Boston and Maine and the Maine Central Railroads for operations on the Rocky Branch.

The agreed-upon secondhand, 60-pound rail arrived that summer of 1907 and construction was begun by contractors Ward and Dowing of Kennebunk, Maine. Seven miles of rail were built up the Rocky Branch valley that year,

TERMS OF THE CONWAY COMPANY AGREEMENT WITH THE MAINE CENTRAL AND BOSTON & MAINE RAILROADS FOR OPERATION OF THE ROCKY BRANCH RAILROAD

The Conway Company, for its part, was to construct the railroad, the signal operator's cabin, and the necessary signals at the junction of the logging railroad with Maine Central. The company was also to erect a water tank up on the Rocky Branch and keep it filled, and build a "wye" at the south end of the construction. The Maine Central would be responsible to remove the snow and ice on the track as far up as they operated on the Rocky Branch, but Conway Company would have to pay them for doing so.

The Boston & Maine and the Maine Central, on the other hand, were to furnish the log cars and motive power, and train their crews to move logs to the Conway sawmill. Conway Company would pay the B&M and MEC according to the volume of logs harvested, and would pay rental for use of the log trucks at $1.25 per thousand board feet of logs. Logs would be measured by the Blodgett Log Rule (also known as the New Hampshire Rule), which allowed 115 cubic feet of log for each one thousand board feet of log. The scale or volume was to be marked on the end of each log and was to be the same scale paid to jobbers who brought the logs to the railside landing.

Conway Company also agreed to supply two loaded trains each day, except on Sundays, with a minimum trainload of eighteen thousand board feet. If less than minimum, they would have to reimburse the railroad company for costs. Conway Company was liable for any injuries, fires and damage to engines and livestock.

The term of the agreement was ten years.

The Storehouse and company store on the Rocky Branch.

The Storehouse area served as a base camp. Note the car-loading skidways on the siding that serves The Storehouse.

Climax No. 5 (first) with crew in front of the Rocky Branch engine house.

stopping at a point near Lower Stairs Brook where the logging headquarters was soon to be built.

Rails were in place and logs should have been cut and hauled railside for the journey down the hill, but the Rocky Branch woods had suddenly become quiet in that summer of 1907; no loggers appeared. It seems that the financial panic of 1907 hit hard on Oakleigh Thorne and his financial institutions that controlled the Conway Company. His financial empire had overextended its investments, failure was threatened, and funds were not available to commence logging.

Thorne's institutions did survive the banking crisis, however, and by late 1908 the Conway Company was again into production. Logging began on the Rocky Branch during that winter of 1908–09. A small settlement, known as The Storehouse, was built at the seven-mile point on the railroad in 1908. The settlement included a large camp building, a company store, and a storage house. A half-mile below, near Stairs Brook, a one-stall engine house and water tank was set up. In October the company transferred Alton Vining to Rocky Branch to manage the store.

The first engine Conway Company sent up to help on the new line in the fall of 1908 was one of the small Baldwin saddletanks, operated by Archie Griffin and Herb Moore, with Tommy Hamilton its conductor. The grade over the first seven miles (from the junction with the Maine Central line to The Storehouse) was not restrictive, being only about 2½ percent. That posed no problem for the little Baldwin.

As was the case along the Swift River, contractors did the logging with their own crews of men. One of the first contractors to set up along the Rocky Branch was actually brought in by another lumbering firm, which also owned timberland in the valley—the Libbys of Gorham. They supplied a

The water tank was located behind the engine house on the Rocky Branch.

Rocky Branch logging camp No. 1.

Wet clothes are hung to dry in front of the bunks in camp No. 1.

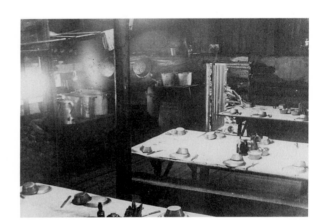

The kitchen and eating tables were located close together in camp No. 1.

The rotund cook of camp No. 1 (second from left) is flanked by his two cookees or helpers. The man on the right was possibly on hand to raid the cookie jar.

large quantity of logs to move out on the railroad. Walter Pittman was one of the first contractors, logging near The Storehouse in 1908, probably for the Libbys.

The horses had an easy pull up Maple Mountain with the cable pulling the sled hitched behind them.

A portion of the Libby timber was over on the east side of the ridge in the Ellis River drainage along Meserve Brook. The distance to the Rocky Branch rail line was not far, but it meant pulling the sled loads of logs up a steep grade and over the height-of-land near Maple Mountain. This was still the best way out, though, and to bring the logs up the steep grade that the horses could never have surmounted with a load, a drum-and-cable hoist was set up on the ridgetop. The 2,700-foot cable was hooked onto the front of the sled at the bottom of the steep grade and, as the load was pulled up, the horses had an easy walk up the hill.

A large logging camp—referred to as Jonesville—was located near The Storehouse, probably a short ways above it. This was also the location of the so-called "pest house," where smallpox victims were once housed.

Three more miles of railroad were built beyond The Storehouse in the spring of 1909 to the foot of the section of the valley where the grade became much steeper. The Libbys built a camp along the rail line where it crossed the Coös–Carroll county line and also the Curtis Camp in Bryants Valley. Contractor Cummings set up his camp at the end of this three-mile extension in 1909. Most of the woodsmen were French Canadian, but there were also a few from Prince Edward Island (PI's). As many as two hundred to three hundred men were in the Rocky Branch woods during the winter months.

In 1910 the final two miles of rail were constructed up the steep grade, terminating almost at the headwaters of the Rocky Branch. At the head end of the railroad, Jim Monahan was directed to set up a camp. These last two

Logging bosses Charlie Sullivan and Dan McGinnis.

A WILD RIDE
DOWN THE ROCKY BRANCH

———◆·◆·◆———

Frank J. Runey, former superintendent of Boston & Maine's Mountain Division, once reminisced about a hair-raising experience he had on the Rocky Branch Railroad. The account was first published in the *Maine Central Railroad Magazine*.

"I was made superintendent of the Mountain Division in 1906, and at that time we had just begun to operate the Rocky Branch. Late in December of that year, I wanted to cover the log job, so I started out of Bartlett with the crew. The track was badly drifted, and we had to plow it out before taking the log bunks up, so it was pretty late when we got to Depot Camp. Then we found that two cars of logs were derailed, and it would be some hours before we could get our train. I had to catch 163 to Portland, so I couldn't wait; and I started to walk down the mountain to Glen station, carrying my bag.

"After walking about half a mile, I saw a section crew's push car beside the track. I looked it over, saw it had a brake, and as it was all down hill, I put the thing on the track, gave it a push and jumped on. I got down on my knees and took hold of the brake lever; and when the speed got up to about 20 miles an hour, I put the brake on, but it wouldn't hold. Then I found that the brake-head was missing. I was going so fast then that I couldn't get off.

"I noticed one of the floor boards was broken, so by pounding with my heel, I managed to split off a small piece which I put between the brake lever and the wheel. That slowed me down a little bit, but then I lost the piece of board and the speed commenced to pick up. I stood up on my feet and took to the air, and landed in a snow drift, end over end. After digging myself out, I remembered that my bag was still on the car.

"I walked along to the main line switch, and saw a couple men there. I asked them if a push car had gone by. 'Yes,' they said, 'it's down there in the gravel pit, upside down and all stove to pieces.' I went down in the pit and found my bag, not damaged much.

"About that time the agent at Glen came up the track, all excited, and said the section men had reported a push car with a man on it, going 60 miles an hour, and that when they found the car they would find a dead man with it.

"Well, I wasn't dead; and I went along to Portland on 163. Just the same, I wouldn't want to take that ride over again!"

The temperature was well down this day as Climax No. 5 arrived at The Storehouse with loaded cars.

sections of track construction, totaling about five miles, climbed a much steeper grade than the first seven miles. The average grade from The Storehouse to the end of the line was 7.5 percent, but there was one section—known as Engine Hill—which surmounted a grade of almost nine percent. The sixty-pound rail used in all of the construction was leased from the Boston and Maine, with the stipulation that the rail be returned to the Glen station within three months of termination.

A few years later, about 1914, the Conway Company built a large siding off the Maine Central main line near Glen, which had no connection to the Rocky Branch operation. Located 2.1 miles east of the Bartlett depot, the 2,000-foot track went southerly up along Stony Brook to apparently provide an outlet for some timber being logged on the flanks of Attitash Mountain. The siding was operated by Maine Central power and removed in October 1917.

Railroad Operations

The first seven miles of the Rocky Branch—the easy grade section that went as far as The Storehouse—were operated by Maine Central power for most, if not all, of the six-year operation. The loaded log trucks were accumulated by Conway Company on a siding at The Storehouse for the two or three trainloads taken down each day by Maine Central during the winter. The loads were hauled to a long siding built just west of Glen Station.

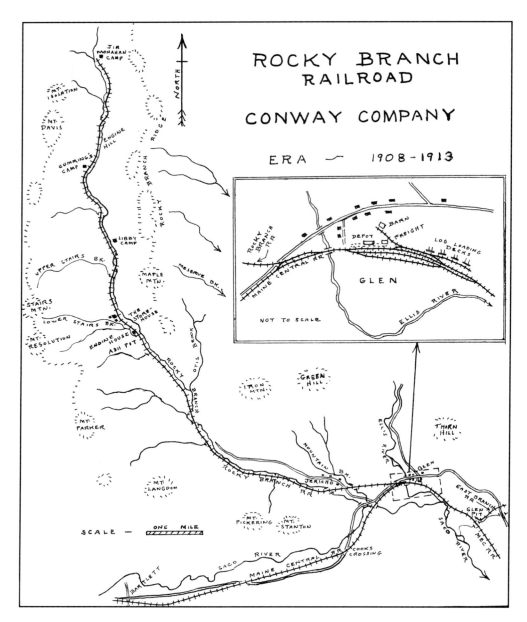

ROCKY BRANCH
RAILROAD

CONWAY COMPANY

ERA — 1908-1913

NORTH

JIM MONAHAN CAMP

MT. ISOLATION

MT. DAVIS

ENGINE HILL

CUMMING'S CAMP

ROCKY BRANCH RIDGE

LIBBY CAMP

UPPER STAIRS BK.

MAPLE MTN.

RESERVE BK.

STAIRS MTN.

LOWER STAIRS BK.

THE STORE HOUSE

MT. RESOLUTION

ENGINE HOUSE

ASH PIT

OTIS BROOK

ROCKY BRANCH

MT. PARKER

IRON MTN.

GREEN HILL

THORN HILL

MT. LANGDON

ROCKY BRANCH RR

JERICHO

MOUNTAIN BK.

ELLIS RIVER

GLEN

EAST BRANCH RR

GLEN PIT

SACO RIVER

MEC. RR

MT. PICKERING

MT. STANTON

COOKS CROSSING

SCALE — ONE MILE

BARTLETT

SACO RIVER

MAINE CENTRAL RR

ROCKY BRANCH RR

DEPOT

BARN

FREIGHT

LOG LOADING DECKS

MAINE CENTRAL RR

GLEN

NOT TO SCALE

ELLIS RIVER

Engine No. 119 was one of the Maine Central locomotives assigned the task of operation on the Rocky Branch. There appears to be a second train following.

One of the engines assigned by the Maine Central to operate the Rocky Branch was No. 224, with engineer Irving E. Currier (later F. W. Littlefield), fireman Ralph Mead, conductor Jack Sloan, and brakeman Willis Rideout. The Maine Central was also responsible for keeping that section plowed out in winter.

From Glen Station, the log train was taken on the Maine Central line to Intervale and then on the Boston and Maine track to the Conway Company

A Maine Central work crew at Glen Station. Identified are George L. Knight (on the left), Walter Parker (far right), and Winfield Chandler (seated).
Courtesy of Bartlett Library

mill. Glen Station had a busy existence during this era. In the winter it was the movement of the log cars and in the summer the departure of traffic for Mt. Washington. It was not uncommon to see one hundred horses with wagons lined up awaiting passengers bound for the mountain area.

Above The Storehouse, the grade on the Rocky Branch was too steep for a rod engine, and this section was operated by the Conway Company with either of the two Climax geared locomotives. The first one was purchased new in 1908 and given the number "5," but was sold two years later to the Brown Company. The second Climax came to the company new in 1910, and since the other Climax had already been sold this new one was also given the number "5." Then, after a serious accident to the second No. 5, the company bought back the first Climax and renumbered it No. 1.

EFFECTIVE SEPTEMBER 26, 1920

MAINE CENTRAL RAILROAD

WINTER SCHEDULE

COMPLETE TIME TABLES

Showing Through Passenger Car Service and Connections

TO AND THROUGH

MAINE NEW HAMPSHIRE VERMONT AND CANADA

PORTLAND, FABYANS, ST. JOHNSBURY and LIME RIDGE

M1374	M1370	M1378	†1154 1224	1166	M1380	†168	Miles	Stations.	1151	M1279	†165	M1383	M1371	†225 †163	M1381
A.M.	A.M.	A.M.	P.M.	P.M.	P.M.	P.M.			A.M.	A.M.	P.M.	A.M.	P.M.	P.M.	P.M.
			†8 45			†3 40	0	Lv Portland Ar	†8 25					†8 30	
	8 55				3 50		4.3	" Cumberland Mills Lv	8 15					8 20	
	9 05				4 00		9.8	" South Windham "	8 04					8 10	
		f9 08			f4 03		10.9	" Newhall "	f7 59					f8 05	
		9 13			4 08		12.5	" White Rock "	7 55					f8 01	
		9 21			4 16		15.6	" Sebago Lake "	7 48					7 55	
		9 24			4 20		17.4	" Smith's Mill "	7 39					7 46	
		f9 28			f4 24		19.3	" Richville "	7 35					f7 42	
		9 35			4 32		23.5	" Steep Falls "	7 28					7 35	
		9 39			4 36		25.3	" Mattocks (E. Baldwin) "	7 23					7 29	
		9 49			4 47		30.6	" Cornish "	7 13					7 17	
		9 54			4 52		32.3	" West Baldwin "	7 10					7 10	
		10 02			4 59		35.2	" Bridgton Jct. "	7 01					7 03	
		10 06			5 03		35.7	" Hiram "	6 56					6 55	
		10 16			5 14		42.2	" Brownfield "	6 46					6 43	
		10 30			5 27		48.7	" Fryeburg "	6 35					6 31	
		10 40			5 37		53.2	" Conway Centre "	6 24					6 20	
		10 46			5 45		55.7	" Redstone "	6 18					6 14	
		10 58			5 53		58.2	" North Conway "	6 12					6 08	
		10 58			6 05		60.3	" Intervale "	6 07					6 03	
		11 05			6 13		63.6	" Glen and Jackson Lv	6 00					5 55	
		11 15			f6 23		69.4	Ar ‖Bartlett ‖	†5 50					5 45	
		11 40					69.4	Lv Ar						5 35	
		11 49					73.7	" Sawyer's River Lv						f5 27	
		f11 53					75.4	" Bemis "						f5 25	
		f12 08					79.8	" Willey House "						5 13	
		12 25					83.9	" Crawford's "						5 02	
		f12 31					87.2	" Bretton Woods "						f4 52	
		12 35					88.0	Ar Fabyan's { Lv						4 50	
		12 35					88.0	Lv { Ar						4 50	
		12 37					88.8	" White Mt. House "						f4 45	
		12 44					92.4	" Twin Mountain Lv						4 38	
		12 50					96.1	" Carroll "						f4 30	
		1 03	14 40	f6 45			98.4	" Quebec Jct. "		†6 10	†12 45			4 25	
		1 10	4 45	f6 52			100.3	Ar Jefferson Jct. { Lv		6 05	12 40			4 15	
		1 10	4 45	f6 52			100.3	Lv { Ar		6 05	12 34			4 15	
		1 15	f4 50	f6 58			103.3	" Bailey's "		6 00	12 29			f4 09	
		f1 21	f4 56	f7 05			106.6	" Riverton "		f5 54	12 23			f4 03	
		1 30	5 05	f7 15			110.3	Ar Lancaster { Lv		15 45	12 15			3 55	
	18 00	1 30	6 05				110.3	Lv { Ar			7 17			3 50	
	8 10	1 35	6 15				111.3	" Coos Junction Lv			7 13			3 47	
	8 25	1 45	6 26				116.4	" Guildhall "			7 03			3 37	
	f8 34		f6 31				119.1	" Stevens "			f6 57				
	8 46	f1 56	f6 39				122.9	" Maidstone "			f6 49			f3 24	
	f8 51	f2 04	f6 45				125.8	" Mason's "			f6 42			f3 16	
	9 40	2 14	6 55				130.9	Ar North Stratford { Lv			6 32			3 06	
	9 40	2 14	7 00				130.9	Lv { Ar			6 27			3 06	
	f9 50	f2 21	f7 07				134.6	" Georges "			f6 20			f2 58	
	f9 58	f2 26	f7 14				137.2	" Cone's "			f6 12			f2 52	
	f10 08	f2 32	f7 20				139.8	" Columbia Bridge "			f6 03			f2 47	
	11 14	2 45	7 30				143.7	" Colebrook "			6 02			2 40	
			f7 42				149.5	" Piper Hill "			f5 41				
		12 00	3 03	7 47			151.7	" W. Stewartstown "			5 36				
		†12 08	3 07	†7 52			153.4	Ar Beecher Falls { Lv			15 30			2 15	
	17 00		3 13				153.4	Lv { Ar						2 09	
	7 05		3 18				154.0	" Hereford (Comins Mill) Lv				13 25		1 59	
	f7 17		f3 25				158.0	" East Hereford "				3 18		1 57	
	7 29		3 33				161.9	" Paquetteville "				f2 53		f1 49	
	f7 47		f3 44				167.7	" Malvina "				2 38		1 41	
	f7 52						169.4	" Auckland "				2 18		1 28	
	8 00		3 53				171.5	" St. Malo "				f2 13			
	f8 05		f3 57				173.3	" Camp Four "				2 03		1 19	
	8 12		4 02				175.6	" St. Isidore "				f1 53		f1 14	
	8 17		4 07				177.3	" Clifton "				f1 35		1 05	
	8 35		4 19				182.5	" Sawyerville "				1 15		12 54	
	f8 43		f4 25				185.4	" Eaton Corner "				1 00		12 46	
	9 05		4 35				189.2	" Cookshire Junc. "				12 48		12 38	
	9 15						192.3	" Pope's "				f11 52		12 28	
	f9 26		f4 47				195.9	" Stoketon "				f11 40		12 21	
	f9 30		f4 51				197.3	" Brookbury "				f11 35		12 18	
	9 50		5 00				202.2	Ar ‖Dudswell Jct. { Lv				11 20		12 08	
	f9 50		f5 05				202.2	Lv { Ar				11 20		11 54	
	f9 55		f5 08				203.3	" Lathrop's Lv				f11 03		f11 52	
	10 00		f5 11				204.7	" Dominion "				f10 59		f11 49	
	10 05		5 15				206.5	Ar Lime Ridge Lv				10 55		11 45	
18 25			†12 57				98.4	Lv Quebec Jct. Ar						14 25	†6 33
f6 30			f1 00				99.9	" Hazen's Lv						f4 13	f6 26
6 40			1 12				102.5	" Whitefield "						4 07	6 16
6 50			1 22				105.7	" Scott's Jct. "						3 57	f6 05
7 05			1 27				108.2	" Lunenburg "						3 52	5 57
7 12			f1 32				110.4	" Fitz Dale "	11 10					3 43	f5 47
7 18			1 37				112.4	" East Concord "	11 02					3 38	f5 42
7 27			f1 43				115.1	" Miles Pond "	10 55					3 32	f5 32
7 38			1 49				118.9	" North Concord "	10 42					3 23	5 22
7 51			2 00				122.1	" Concord "	10 30					3 14	5 07
8 05			2 10				125.9	" East St Johnsbury "	9 55					3 05	4 53
†8 18			12 20				130.2	Ar St. Johnsbury Lv	†9 40					12 55	†4 40
A.M.	A.M.	P.M.	P.M.	P.M.	P.M.	P.M.			A.M.	A.M.	P.M.	A.M.	P.M.	P.M.	P.M.

The first Climax No. 5 to operate on the Rocky Branch line was almost new and still bore the factory paint and lettering when this photo was taken at The Storehouse. The number on the front end plate was painted on and didn't last long due to the heat from the smoke box. The boiler had a tapered shell rather than a straight barrel or flat top.

The second Climax, purchased new in 1910, was also numbered "5" because the first one had been sold to the Brown Company. The boiler on this locomotive had a straight shell. Note that the fuel tank is higher than standard. The previous Climax possibly had trouble carrying enough fuel for a day's run, and this engine was ordered with the extra carrying capacity.

Spruce logs were loaded by hand onto the bunk cars. Each pair was connected by a "reach" or connector, and a longer reach was used between each carload.

Logs were loaded on log trucks, which had a 6" × 6" spruce reach joining each pair of trucks, the reach sometimes being as much as eighteen feet long. Most of the one hundred log trucks were leased from the Maine Central Railroad, including a few which still showed the lettering for the Somerset (Maine) Railroad. About twenty-four loaded cars would be gathered at The Storehouse for each trainload for the Maine Central engine. The logs averaged sixty feet in length.

The crew on the company train consisted of four men—the engineer, fireman and the two brakemen—who rode the engine cab going in as the engine backed up with empties, but rode the loaded cars going out. At the top of the steep grade, the engineer would stop on the way out and whistle for the brakemen to run along and set the hand brakes on each car. There were no air

The log trucks can be noted under the jackstraw pile of the spruce logs.

brakes. It appears that the logs were possibly left on these same log cars for the complete trip to the Conway sawmill. But since these cars had no air brakes, it is now difficult to understand how they were allowed over the tracks of the Maine Central or the Boston and Maine. There was no known provision or location to reload the logs onto other cars.

Minor accidents were frequent on the upper end of the Rocky Branch because of the steep nature of the track. If a log truck became disabled, it was pushed off to the side of the track, eventually to be picked up by the company crane when it was in the area. A coupler pin came out on one occasion near the engine house, and fifty sets of log trucks rolled down the lower section of the Rocky Branch and piled up in a pasture down below.

The steep grade just above mile point 10—known as Engine Hill—was the most feared, with a grade of nine percent, probably more in some spots. The tracks had to be sanded all the way down. Once the engine slid off the track for a short distance and engineer Fred Lane was able to jack it back on again with the help of a pair of horses. It was on Engine Hill, however, that a real "hair raiser" occurred.

The date was March 7, 1913, and activities on the Rocky Branch were about to come to a close for the season. The crew was working the Climax on the steep grade when somehow the locomotive got out of control, picking up speed with no chance of braking the descent. The crew had no choice but to "take to the birds," and they leaped. Uninjured were engineer Fred Lane, fire-

The Climax lies in a ruined heap, but the fortunate crew poses uninjured on top of the wreckage. From the left: fireman James Lane, engineer Fred A. Lane, brakeman Albert LaRoache, and conductor Frank Chisholm. The clown below them remains unidentified.

James Lane and Albert LaRoache ponder where they might have been if they hadn't leaped.

man James Lane, conductor Frank Chisholm and brakeman Herb LaRoache. But the Climax lay in a heap of ruins down below. The company sent the demolished Climax off to the Portland Company for repair, but one report has it that the locomotive never operated satisfactorily after the repair work because of the Portland Company's unfamiliarity with a Climax locomotive.

Reportedly a good quantity of logs was abandoned railside, because no other locomotive could negotiate the grade and that was the company's only Climax at the time. The Rocky Branch operations were about to terminate, and this was apparently a clean-up duty that the Climax was undertaking.

Following its repair, Climax No. 5 is photographed in the Portland Company yard. The cab is higher and different than the original one, and dents in the side of the tank are still visible. The line shafts underneath are disconnected, revealing that the engine is ready for transit home, hauled as a dead engine with a required man in the cab.

Members of the Appalachian Mountain Club are assisted aboard a flat car for a 1914 excursion ride up the Rocky Branch.

Over the years fire plagued the Rocky Branch operation much more so than on Swift River. The period 1912–14 saw fires each year, the worst being in the summer of 1912. In late summer that year the Climax was up at the height-of-land picking up logs, the crew consisting of conductor Dan Brackett, engineer Fred Lane and brakeman Albert LaRoache. They had given a ride to a couple of fishermen who had gotten off at Henderson's Camp and started down the river. The train later returned a short way back down the hill to a landing and waited while the landing crew was loading some more cars. The train crew was sitting on the bank and suddenly saw a small fire. At the same time LaRoache saw the fishermen running down the river. A gust of wind fanned the flames and soon the riverbank was engulfed in a roaring fire.

Tom Crowler, fire patrolman for the New Hampshire Timberland Owners Association, was in the area and had the crew take the train down to the next

The scene of devastation at the upper end of the Rocky Branch valley in Sargents Purchase remained for a number of years until a new growth of trees slowly renewed the landscape. The original stand of old-growth spruce here was first logged, then burned over by an intense forest fire.

camp, drop off the cars, and then hurry down to The Storehouse where they could telephone for help. Lane then took the engine down to Glen, picked up a flatcar, and returned to Cannell's Crossing where a large group of firefighters was waiting to be taken up the valley. The fire lasted for twelve days, kept as many as three thousand men on the fire line, and burned over thirty-five thousand acres plus a large quantity of logs.

In June 1914 there was a fire in the buildings up on the Rocky Branch, and the company sent up a large crew of firefighters from the sawmill to squelch the blaze. The U.S. Forest Service examiner later estimated that 57 percent of the Rocky Branch watershed had been burned over. The clearcutting of spruce timber had left a forest floor littered with dry fuel.

The tenure of the Rocky Branch railroad and logging operation was undoubtedly cut short by these fires. The company removed what logs it could, picked up the equipment, and later in the summer and fall of 1914 removed all of the rails on the Rocky Branch Railroad.

The East Branch Railroad (1916–1920)

As the Conway Company's large operation on Swift River was winding down, the company suddenly found itself in a market of inflated lumber prices due to the ongoing world war, and realized that it needed a further source of timber in order to cash in on the wartime boom. The Rocky Branch operation had a disappointing demise in 1914 and the available timber was just about gone in the Swift River valley.

A number of land purchases along the East Branch of the Saco River had

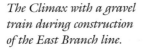

The Climax with a gravel train during construction of the East Branch line.

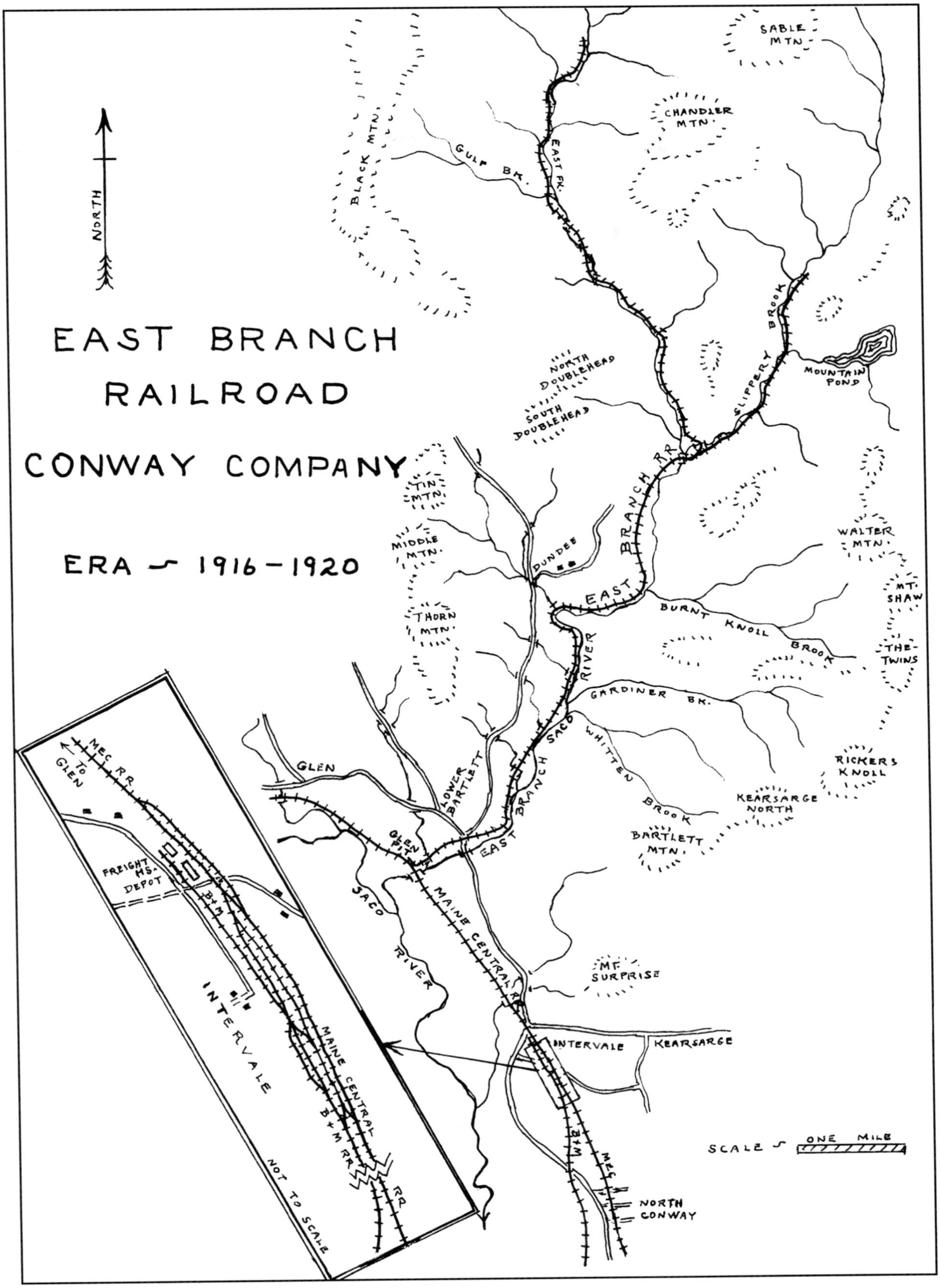

EAST BRANCH
RAILROAD
CONWAY COMPANY

ERA ~ 1916-1920

NORTH

SCALE ~ ONE MILE

SABLE MTN

CHANDLER MTN

EAST FK.

GULF BK.

BLACK MTN

SLIPPERY BROOK

MOUNTAIN POND

NORTH DOUBLEHEAD

SOUTH DOUBLEHEAD

EAST BRANCH R.R.

TIN MTN

DUNDEE

WALTER MTN

MT SHAW

MIDDLE MTN

THORN MTN

EAST BRANCH SACO RIVER

BURNT KNOLL BROOK

THE TWINS

GARDINER BK.

GLEN

LOWER BARTLETT

RICKERS KNOLL

WHITTEN BROOK

KEARSARGE NORTH

GLEN JCN

EAST BRANCH SACO

BARTLETT MTN

SACO RIVER

MAINE CENTRAL

MT SURPRISE

INTERVALE   KEARSARGE

TO GLEN

MEC RR

FREIGHT HS. DEPOT

INTERVALE

MAINE CENTRAL

B+M RR

R.P.

NOT TO SCALE

B+M R.R.

MEC R.R.

NORTH CONWAY

previously been consolidated to form an area that contained a fine cut of timber. Now that lumber prices had taken such an upturn during to the war, the company moved quickly to set up a new area for railroad logging. Also goading them on was the presence of representatives from the U.S. Forest Service seeking land purchases for the new national forest in the White Mountains.

The Swift River Railroad shut down in 1916 and, as the rails were being yanked up on that line at the rate of about a half-mile a day, other rail was being laid along the East Branch. To hurry the construction along, the company had the contractor work from both ends of the surveyed location, moving in men and supplies over the Bald Land Trail from Jackson to reach the upper end.

The first four miles of the new track were over other privately owned properties, and temporary right-of-ways had to be purchased from a half dozen property owners. But it was not a difficult line to construct and there were not the steep grades they had encountered on the Rocky Branch. The overall grade for the thirteen miles built along the East Branch was about 2.5 percent.

By this date the Conway Company had both Climax locomotives again, if needed, to work the East Branch. The first No. 5 had been purchased back from the Brown Company, after use on the Millsfield Railroad, and was renumbered as No. 1. The second No. 5 had been repaired after its accident and was again in use, although not satisfactorily, according to one report. The East Branch Railroad junctioned with the Maine Central at a spot known as Glen Pit, about 1¼ miles southeasterly of Glen Station. In November 1916 the Conway Company built a storehouse and engine house for the Climax at Glen Pit.

The Conway Company's Climax operated the entire length of the East Branch line, leaving the loaded cars on a siding at Glen Pit. As with the Rocky Branch operation, the Maine Central moved the cars to the Intervale exchange

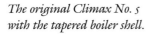

The original Climax No. 5 with the tapered boiler shell.

The second Climax No. 5 on the way out of the woods.

The second Climax No. 5 was eventually sold to the Great Northern Paper Company and taken on a boat trip up a lake.

A team with a loaded bobsled waits patiently at Wilbur Marshall's camp.

and the Boston and Maine to the mill in Conway, about twenty-five cars to a trainload.

Logging on the East Branch was done under the control of contractor Wilbur Marshall, known as Marshall Lumber Company. According to locomotive engineer Eddie Parent, wartime conscientious objectors were taken in to work in the logging camps.

Before the East Branch operation finished up, the Conway Company also set up another operation to hurriedly harvest the timber on some other land of the Publishers Paper Company on the flanks of Wildcat Ridge in the northern edge of the town of Jackson. Wilbur Marshall was the contractor on this job also, which lasted from 1918 to 1920. There was no feasible way of building a railroad to this stand of prime spruce timber, so it was hauled by sled all the way down to Glen Station, where it was loaded on cars on a Maine Central siding. The sled haul covered a strenuous distance of 10–12 miles from Wildcat, long enough to allow only one trip per day for each team.

Harry Marsh of Colebrook had charge of the horses and stated that they had about two hundred horses in the woods. One hundred of them were used on the long sled road down to Glen. Both six-horse and four-horse teams

A four-horse team waits at Wildcat Ridge on the Wilbur Marshall job while the sled is being loaded.

hauled the sleds. Some of the teamsters were older men and were given the four-horse teams because six horses were too much for them to handle.

The East Branch was the last of the Conway Company logging operations, closing down about 1920. The saws in the big sawmill stopped turning in the spring of 1920 after cleaning up the large piles of logs in the yard. The mill buildings were sold in 1923 to R. F. Harman and Company, who operated a box shop on the premises for a few years before the building burned or was torn down. In 1948 the Kennett Corp. built a smaller sawmill on the same site. This stayed in operation until 1960.

The Conway Company kindling mill had burned down in 1915 and was

A six-horse team passes through Jackson on its way from Wildcat Ridge to Glen Station.

The logs were rolled off the sled onto a high bank above the railroad tracks just east of the Glen depot.

The flatcars are loaded and ready for transport. Glen Station is visible on the far left.

afterwards re-established in the old box shop along the B&M tracks. When the sawmill shut down in 1920, the kindling mill also closed its doors. The nearby spool mill on West Main Street continued operations for a few more years. It was owned in its later life by a couple of men who were prominent with the activities of Conway Company, L. D. Goulding and Wilbur Marshall. On January 4, 1934, fire also put an end to this once important village industry.

Thirteen years of railroading through the spruce woods and operating one of the largest sawmills ever built in the Northeast has left many indentations still to be found in Conway and the nearby forested areas. Slowly, however, nature is reclaiming and erasing the evidence of a once intense and busy industry.

CHAPTER SIX

The Wealth of the White Mountains

WE'VE BEEN CONSIDERING an era when the White Mountains region of New Hampshire offered a tempting and seemingly endless supply of prime spruce for the timber barons; too tempting to pass by in preference for any areas that might have easier access. With the unlimited market available for spruce lumber—and the construction industry demanding more and more lumber products—the mountains of northern New Hampshire, Vermont and Maine were cut heavily with little consideration for resulting fire hazards or aesthetics. The public response was predictable: a flood of outrage over the transformation of a forested vacation retreat into what appeared to the public to be a land of inexcusable devastation.

Timber barons such as Oakleigh Thorne and his Conway Lumber Company, George James and his New Hampshire Land Company, and James E. Henry made their fortunes in the only manner understood or practiced by the woodsmen during this era. And any lumbermen of smaller stature also treated the forests in a similar fashion, only on a smaller scale. Even the occasional lumber king who was championed for conservative cutting, though extending the harvest over a longer period, seldom exited a timber tract leaving a final appearance any different from that of a hasty cut-and-get-out operator. Thus the normal and industry-accepted practices of the lumbermen in the virgin timber growth clashed with the ideals of a public enthralled by their mountain retreats.

As far back as 1885 a spark of protest was ignited in the White Mountains regarding the wholesale harvest of the old-growth spruce and the forest fires that sometimes resulted. Emerging from the protest in 1901 was the Society for the Protection of New Hampshire Forests, an organization that deserves

The slash on Mt. Carrigain was five years old when the land was being inspected by (from left to right) chief of U.S Forest Service Henry S. Graves, White Mountain National Forest Supervisor J. J. Fritz, district forester Franklin Reed, SPNHF forester Philip Ayers, Boston Transcript *reporter Allen Chamberlain, and district ranger C. B. Shiffer.*

much of the credit for encouraging the early establishment of national forests in the Northeast.

Legislation to authorize eastern national forests was introduced in 1909 by John Weeks, a congressman from Massachusetts and native of New Hampshire. But some legislators in Washington hotly opposed the move, and it wasn't until 1911 that the Weeks Act was passed. The Weeks Act authorized the use of public monies for the purchase of privately owned timberlands. Only in this way, it was felt, could there be a continuity of ownership and management.

Purchases of cut-over forest land began immediately for the White Mountain National Forest; the initial purchase was 38,000 acres from Berlin Mills Company, later the Brown Company. By the following year, there was over 72,000 acres in the new national forest and 106,000 acres by 1915. For the first few years the land purchases were almost entirely cut-over parcels, arranged by representatives of the U.S. Forest Service as they made contacts with all of the larger lumber operators.

A great majority of the thousands of acres logged over by the Saco River valley railroad loggers also became part of the newly formed White Mountain National Forest. The U.S. Forest Service approached the Conway Company even before they had finished the harvest of the Swift River country; as per custom of the time, Conway Company made an effort to cut as much merchantable timber as possible before deeding the land to the White Mountain

National Forest in about 1917. The Rocky Branch and East Branch valleys were also eventually deeded to the government.

The lands of the Bartlett Land and Lumber Company became part of the White Mountain National Forest about the same time. In 1931, the Bartlett Experimental Forest was established, setting aside twenty-six hundred acres for experimental studies. Included in the Experimental Forest were several areas of still-existing old-growth hardwood trees.

In the early 1930s the Dry River valley was purchased by the U.S. government and is now the principal portion of the Presidential–Dry River Wilderness area. The upper half of the Rocky Branch valley is also included within this wilderness designation. There will be no future timber harvests in this area.

The Sawyer River country was the last of the tracts logged by railroad to become part of the White Mountain National Forest. The U.S. Forest Service had expressed an interest in purchasing the land as far back as 1918, but did not offer a price deemed satisfactory by the heirs of Charles G. Saunders. Discussions and offers were made during the ensuing years, but not until 1937 did the government purchase the 29,900 acres. Included in the purchase was a patch of virgin spruce at the head end of Nancy Brook, with some spruce as old as 390 years and some balsam fir determined to be as old as 202 years (as of 1975). This old-growth timber is now set aside as the Nancy Brook Research Natural Area.

Horace Currier was the first forest ranger to serve in the district covering the Saco River. He was forest ranger there from 1916 to 1920. His truck was the first Forest Service vehicle on the White Mountain National Forest.

Patches of darker green spruce can be noted today among the lighter colored deciduous trees in the Swift River valley.

What are the woods like today on the mountainsides that once grew such a thick blanket of spruce? That former forest growth that was once so heavy throughout with spruce does not exist at present. After being clearcut, it's usually the nature of northeastern spruce stands to regenerate with hardwood trees. Spruce has difficulty competing with a sudden profusion of hardwood sprouts. And it's suspected that conditions favoring the establishment of spruce were much more favorable in the distant past. But spruce seed will establish under a hardwood overstory after ten years or so, and many patches of healthy spruce can be noticed on these hillsides that were once clearcut by the railroad loggers. Small spruce and fir are plentiful on the upper slopes.

Have the hillsides of the White Mountains become devastated or ruined, as was so often predicted after the severe cuttings by the railroad loggers? Not at all. The forests have a wonderful capacity to regenerate, to come back, and rebound and renew themselves, even after a tough lashing. There were a number of follow-up timber sales conducted in the Swift River area in the 1950s and 1960s, set up by the forest management staff at the local U.S. Forest Service ranger station. There have likewise been timber harvests in the Bartlett area and in Sawyer River area, starting in the late 1950s. Forests are a renewable resource.

No, the mountains were not made bare, and the rivers did not dry up in the wake of the loggers wielding axes and crosscut saws. Even those valleys burned to a crisp by the ruinous forest fires have long since turned green with the next generation of trees.

The lumber barons performed their tasks and made their fortunes as per customs of that era, wasteful as they sometimes were to the forest. The railroads had come into the North Country at the most opportune time, just when needed to pull out the greatest harvest of logs those mountains will ever give up. Then those severe harvests of the timber barons unwittingly created the climate that put the mountains into public domain. The forests remain, as healthy as ever; the railroad loggers have steamed off into oblivion.

Glossary

BOBSLED—A single set of sled runners with a cross beam on top upon which the front end of the log is placed while the rear end drags on the ground.

BOARD FOOT—A piece of lumber 12 inches long, 12 inches wide and 1 inch thick, or one of equivalent cubic volume.

CANT DOG—A basic woodsmen's tool for turning or prying logs; consists of a long handle with a spike on the end and a hook near the end.

CHOPPER—The member of the logging crew who fells trees and cuts them into logs.

CIRCULAR SAWMILL—A mill using a large circular saw for the principle break-down of the log into lumber.

CLEARCUTTING—Cutting all of the trees in the forest or in some cases, just cutting all of the merchantable trees.

COMMON CARRIER—A railroad chartered and authorized by the government to carry passengers.

COOKEE—A camp cook's helper or assistant.

CORD—A pile of wood four feet long, eight feet wide and four feet high, or a pile of equivalent cubic volume.

CROSSCUT SAW—A two-man saw, generally about 5½ feet long, used to cut trees.

FLANGER—The metal scraper mounted under a railroad car used to remove snow and ice from between the rails.

GEARED LOCOMOTIVE—Any engine that had the power from the cylinders transmitted to the wheels by means of gears.

HARDWOOD TREES—Deciduous trees, those which shed their leaves each fall; in the White Mountains, especially beech, birch, maple, and ash.

JOBBER—A logging contractor or subcontractor.

LANDING—Location where logs from the woods are accumulated for rolling into a river or loading onto sleds or railroad cars.

LINK-AND-PIN COUPLERS—An old style of coupling railroad cars together in which a link, generally an oval metal ring, is secured in the pocket on the ends of adjoining cars by heavy metal pins.

LOG RULE—A measurement formula used to determine the estimated quantity of board feet that can be sawn from a log. The Blodgett, or New Hampshire, Rule was the official rule recognized in the state of New Hampshire.

MERCHANTABLE—That portion of a timber stand or of a tree that can be logged profitably and have a market to which it can be sold.

OLD GROWTH—Virgin timber, never been logged.

RAIL WEIGHT—Measurement based on the number of pounds per yard of rail.

RIGHT-OF-WAY—The legally obtained strip of land within which the railroad track or road is built.

ROD LOCOMOTIVES—The standard type of locomotive with the main drive rod from the piston attached directly to a drive wheel.

SADDLETANK—A locomotive with the water tank over the boiler, saddle fashion, eliminating the need for a tender.

SCALING—Measuring the board feet or cord content of logs or trees.

SKIDDING—Hauling logs on the ground without use of sled runners.

SKID ROAD—A cleared path over which horses dragged logs to the landing.

SKIDWAY—Elevated cribwork from which logs were loaded on railroad cars or sleds.

SNUBBING—The use of cable or ropes to regulate the descent of loaded sleds on steep slopes.

SOFTWOOD TREES—Conifers, with needles; in the White Mountains, especially pine, spruce, fir and hemlock.

STUMPAGE—Refers to standing trees.

TENDER —The car attached to the rear of a locomotive, carrying water and fuel.

TRACK FROGS —The point in a rail switch where the train wheels cross to another rail, having depressed channels to allow passage of the wheel flangers. It is so named because of the resemblance to a part of a horse's hoof which bears the same name.

TRESPASS (TIMBER) —The unlawful cutting of trees belonging to another owner.

TRUCK (RAILROAD) —Framework under a car that holds the axles and flanged wheels; generally two axles.

TWO SLED —Two independent sets of sled runners connected by a set of cross chains.

WALKING BOSS —Foreman in charge of two or more logging camps, usually walking between them.

YARDING —The assembling of logs in one place for loading.

Bibliography

Albany Centennial. Albany, N.H. 1966.

Beale, Charles Edward Jr. *Passaconaway in the White Mountains*. Boston: Richard G. Badger. 1916.

Belcher, Francis C. *Logging Railroads of the White Mountains*. Boston: Appalachian Mountain Club. 1980.

Bolles, Frank. *At the North of Bearcamp Water*. Boston: Houghton Mifflin Company. 1893.

Carroll, Aileen M. *In the Valley of the Saco*. Bartlett, N.H.: Bartlett Public Library. 1990.

Chaney, Michael P. *White Pine on the Saco River*. Orono, Maine: Maine Folklife Center. 1990.

Chittenden, Alfred K. *Forest Conditions of Northern New Hampshire*. USDA Bureau Forestry Bulletin No. 55. 1905.

Eastman, M. E. *East of the White Hills*. 1900.

Horne, Ruth. *Conway Through the Years and Whither*. Conway, N.H.: Conway Historical Society. 1963.

Kilbourne, Frederick W. *Chronicles of the White Mountains*. Boston: Houghton Mifflin Company. 1916.

Maine Central Mountain Division. Portland, Maine: 470 Railroad Club. 1985.

Meader, J. W. *The Merrimack River*. Boston: B. B. Russell. 1869.

Merrill, Georgia Drew. *History of Carroll County*. 1889.

Morris, George F. *Reminiscences of a Yankee Jurist*. 1953.

Perry, A. Bernard. *Albany's Recollections*. Albany, N.H. 1976.

Poole, Ernest. *The Great White Hills of New Hampshire*. New York: Doubleday and Company, Inc. 1946.

Sweeter, Moses F. *Osgood's White Mountains*. Boston: James R. Osgood and Company. 1876.

Varney, Marion L. *Hart's Location in Crawford Notch*. Portsmouth, N.H.: Peter E. Randall. 1997.

PERIODICALS

American Lumberman, 1905–1921

Among the Clouds, July 18, 1876

Conway Reporter, 1907–1909

Forestry, Irrigation and Conservation, Feb. 1908

New Hampshire Forestry Commission Annual Reports, 1890–1906

North Country Reporter, 1914, 1916

Northwestern Lumberman, Feb. 1887

Poors, 1892–1893

Southern Lumberman, Nov. 1911

White Mountain Echo, Sept. 14, 1895

White Mountain Reporter, 1902

Index

Page numbers in italics refer to illustrations.

About the Author

Bill Gove is a retired forester with a deep interest in forest history, as well as the histories of lumbering and railroading. He is the author of numerous magazine articles and the co-author of the books *Rails in the North Woods* and *Vermont's Granite Railroads*. In 1998 he also authored the book *J. E. Henry's Logging Railroads*. Retired from the Vermont Department of Forests and Parks, he resides year-round in Williamstown, Vermont.